How to Administer an Estate in Ontario

Plain Language Handbook for the Executor / Estate Trustee

Lead author:
John Allen, B.A., B.Sc., LL.B., LL.M., Ph.D. (law)

Contributing author – law
Adam Malek, B.A., Juris Doctor (J.D.)

Contributing authors – income tax
Brian J. Quinlan, C.P.A., C.A., C.F.P., T.E.P.
Dickson Lai, C.P.A., C.A., T.E.P.

Notice and Disclaimer

ISBN: 979-8-6765-9358-2

Cover image by Zoë Paige Allen

Preface

This handbook is for those who have been appointed an executor (now called an "estate trustee") in Ontario. It tells you what needs to be done, when to do it, what you can do yourself, and when you should seek the assistance of a lawyer or an accountant. It is an easy to read, plain language, guide.

It was written in August 2020. There are few footnotes. The relevant statutes are available on the Ontario e-laws website ontario.ca/laws: *Estate Administration Tax Act, Estates Act, Estates Administration Act, Family Law Act, Succession Law Reform Act,* and the *Trustee Act.* For income tax issues, the federal *Income Tax Act* is relevant.

It was a collaborative effort. John Allen and Adam Malek are estate lawyers at the Toronto firm of Allen & Allen. Brian J. Quinlan and Dickson Lai are chartered professional accountants at the Toronto firm of Campbell Lawless LLP.

With special thanks to Pearson Allen for his research skills, and to Eileen Barnes, who helped edit the draft with her extensive experience in estate administration.

Contents

Introduction

This handbook is for those who have been appointed an executor (now called an "estate trustee") in Ontario. When someone close to you has died, leaving you in charge of all their worldly possessions, and when others are also grieving and looking to you to settle things quickly and fairly, you need a plain language guide. This is that guide. It is divided into chapters, corresponding to the stages in the administration of the estate. It tells you what needs to be done, when to do it, what you can do yourself, and when you should seek the assistance of a lawyer or accountant.

The estate you are about to administer may look simple. It may be your mother's, who was living in a nursing home, all her assets were invested in a balanced portfolio, and the remainder is to be divided equally between you and your sister. What can go wrong? The answer is, you don't know yet. As you follow the stages in the administration of her estate, you will learn that her unpaid debts, her personal income taxes, and the estate's income taxes are your responsibility. You may need to defend against a dependant support claim, or allegations that her will did not express her true wishes. You need to sleep at night, so use this handbook as a guide, and seek professional advice when necessary.

Some estate administration decisions can be difficult:

- How should personal possessions, like jewelry and paintings, be divided among the beneficiaries?

- What should you do with assets that have emotional values? For some, the family cottage, with childhood memories, where friendships and rivalries formed, where private thoughts were revealed, cannot be immediately sold for cash without hurt feelings within the family.

- What should you do with the family business? It may be difficult to value a family business if one child joined their parent entrepreneur while the others sought careers elsewhere. What is the value of an entrepreneurial business without its founder?

- What if the deceased accumulated wealth and remarried late in life, and he, her second husband, who she loved, but who always floundered and who was financially dependent on her - should her children from her prior marriage receive more than his children from his prior marriage when they both die?

- How should you administer testamentary trusts, such as trusts for young children, the surviving spouse, an adult child with a mental disability or substance concern, or a child with financial difficulties?

- How should you handle litigation? Sometimes, the surviving spouse will make a family law division claim or a spousal support claim. One of the children may claim dependant support. A former business associate could file a claim. Or, the estate may have a claim against the spouse, child, or business associate, for compensation, or that certain assets should revert to the estate which you, as estate trustee, have a duty to pursue.

There is a lot that can go wrong when administering an estate. This handbook doesn't have all the answers, but it deals with the most common issues that can arise, and, if there are surprises, it points you in the right direction.

This handbook was written in August 2020 and it applies to Ontario, Canada estates. We have used plain language where possible. For example, we have used "will-maker" rather than "testator" or "testatrix". Also, we have used "their" for singular possessive, rather than "his or her", and we have used "they" rather than "he or she".

Chapter One—First Steps

This chapter highlights the most pressing responsibilities, such as funeral and burial arrangements; gathering and reviewing important documents; caring for children and dependants; terminating leases; terminating licenses; terminating subscriptions and memberships; and documenting assets and liabilities.

The funeral

Your first responsibility is to arrange the funeral and the burial or cremation.

You are not legally bound to follow the funeral or burial wishes expressed in the deceased's will,[1] but you should honour them as much as possible. Sometimes, people pre-arrange and pre-pay their funeral; if so, you should meet with the funeral director, pick a date for the service, draft the obituary, and follow the deceased's wishes. Funeral expenses, if reasonable when compared to the funds available in the estate, must be paid before other debts.

You should inform family and friends of the death as soon as possible. You can search for contacts in email accounts, cell phone records, and personal telephone books. Contact the employer and organizations that the deceased belonged to, if necessary.

Inform close family members who wish to travel to the funeral that some airlines offer reduced prices, known as bereavement fares.

---

[1] *Williams v. Williams* [1882] 20 ChD 659

It can be an emotional time to draft the obituary, plan the service, and arrange the burial. The funeral director can guide you and arrange for publishing the obituary in the local paper or on its website, with details of the service. Know that the other administrative tasks can wait until the service is completed. There is no need to distribute a copy of the will at this stage, nor is there a "reading of the will" as you may have seen in the movies. After the funeral, you can send copies of the will to the beneficiaries. See below. For now, concentrate on paying your respects and dealing with the loss.

Gift of organs or tissue

The deceased may have included a provision in their will or other document expressing an intention that their organs or tissue be donated for transplants or medical research. Under Ontario's *Trillium Gift of Life Network Act,* any person who has attained the age of sixteen years may consent, in writing signed by the person at any time or orally in the presence of a least two witnesses during the person's last illness, that the person's body, or parts of their body, be used after their death for therapeutic purposes, medical education or scientific research. If they have died, their spouse, or if the spouse is not readily available, their children, or if the children are also not readily available, the deceased's siblings can give consent. In some cases, another person in lawful possession of the body can give consent.

Burial and spreading the ashes

In Ontario, the body or cremated remains must be buried in a licensed cemetery. Rights to bury or scatter the ashes in a designated part of the cemetery can be purchased, though scattering rights are not available at all cemeteries. You can buy rights to place the cremated remains in a niche (or compartment) in a columbarium. You may scatter the ashes on private property with the written consent of the landowner. You may also scatter the ashes on unoccupied Crown lands and Crown lands covered by water, if there are no signs prohibiting the scattering of remains.

Writing the obituary and giving a eulogy

The funeral director will help you write the obituary, which is the notice of death, often published in the local newspaper. Standard information includes the deceased's age and date of death. A short biography can follow, including place of birth, education, vocation, and significant life events. Then, a list of family by name, including the spouse, children, parents, siblings, and close relatives, and those who have predeceased. Grandchildren can be named, or mentioned as "survived by six grandchildren, four nieces," etc. Contact information for a charitable foundation or society to direct any memorial donations can be listed. Details of any funeral service should be included.

A eulogy is a speech given at a service in memory of the deceased. It needn't be long, probably three to five minutes. The tone will depend on who gives it and the circumstances of the death. One for a teenager who met an untimely death will be different than one for someone who died peacefully at an old age. Briefly introduce yourself and your connection to the deceased, state some basic information, welcome those who have attended, and then tell a story or incident that illustrates the deceased's good qualities and why the deceased was important in your life. Write what you wish to say ahead of time and arrange with a friend to read your speech if you become too emotional or nervous to deliver it yourself.

Gather the documents

Locate important documents, including:

- The original will (or wills, if there is a primary and secondary will);
- Affidavit of the witness who saw the signing of the will ("affidavit of execution");
- Any notes or memos the deceased may have left with their will;
- Any notes or lists of the deceased's assets;
- Death certificates, issued by the funeral home;
- Details of any insurance policies;
- Deceased's income tax returns and income tax information slips; and
- Details of any safety deposit box.

Safety deposit box

If the safety deposit box is held only in the name of the deceased, the financial institution should allow you, as the estate trustee, to examine the contents. Usually the institution will not allow the removal of the contents (except the will) until a Certificate of Appointment of Estate Trustee (i.e. probate) is obtained, or a notarized copy of the will is produced along with an indemnity by the estate trustee to compensate the institution against claims related to any wrongful removal of the contents.

Sending copies of the will to the beneficiaries

You should send copies of the will, or extracts of the will, to the beneficiaries after the funeral. If, however, you anticipate that you will need probate (a "Certificate of Appointment of Estate Trustee With a Will"—see chapter four), then you could wait. As part of the probate application, you will be required to send copies, so you could wait until then to avoid duplication.

The legacy beneficiaries should be sent copies of only the relevant clauses. For example, if a beneficiary is to receive a $5,000 gift, then you could write to the beneficiary and state that the deceased's will includes a gift of $5,000, which will be sent as soon as the administration of the estate has reached the stage of a distribution.

The residuary beneficiaries who are to receive a percentage or share of the estate should receive copies of the entire will, because the amount that they will receive depends on who else is receiving and what the debts and costs of the estate will be. If you wish, you could estimate the value of the estate, or you could state that you will be sending an estimate in due course.

Young children and dependants

Is there a clause in the will about who should have custody of the deceased's young children? The appointment is binding only for 90 days. The court retains the authority to appoint a guardian thereafter. However, the expressed wishes of a parent in their will is an important factor for the court to consider in the event that there is any dispute beyond the 90 days.

Do the children or other dependants need immediate access to funds? If so, you should make financial arrangements if possible.

Cancel health card, passport and driver's license

You should return the Ontario health card to the Ontario Ministry of Health and the deceased's passport to the Passport Program, Gatineau, Quebec, K1A 0G3.

Apply for a refund for the driver's license if there are six months or more remaining before it expires and there are no outstanding fines. An "Application for Refund of Driver's Licence" form cancels the driver's licence and requests a refund of the licence fee, if applicable. You must return the original, plastic licence card.[2]

---

[2] Service Ontario: <https://www.ontario.ca/page/get-refund-or-credit-your-licence-plate-sticker-or-drivers-licence>

Cancel credit cards, cell phone contracts, subscriptions, and forward mail

Cancel: (i) the deceased's credit cards, (ii) cell phone contracts, (iii) refilling prescriptions, (iv) utilities, unless heat and water are required to maintain a property, (v) memberships, (vi) newspaper, magazine and online subscriptions, and (vii) any online accounts.

Arrange for mail forwarding to your personal address.

Advise Canada Revenue Agency of the death

Canada Revenue Agency ("CRA") should be informed of the death as soon as possible. This can be done by calling 1-800-959-8281. The deceased's social insurance number will be needed. An alternative to calling is to complete the form in the CRA's information sheet RC4111 "What to do following a death" and sending it to your nearest tax centre. A copy of the death certificate should be sent with the notification of death. The notification will stop, as applicable:

- The Harmonized Sales Tax ("HST") tax credit payments;
- Ontario Trillium payments
- Canada child benefit payments

Advise Service Canada of the death

Service Canada manages the Canada Pension Plan (CPP) and Old Age Security (OAS) payments. Service Canada should be informed promptly of the date of death to avoid overpayments which would otherwise need to be repaid. Benefits paid for the month in which the death occurs can be kept, but benefits received for later months must be returned. Service Canada can be contacted by telephone at 1-800-622-6232 and they will provide the address of their closest office. As with CRA, the initial correspondence with Service Canada should include a copy of the deceased's death certificate.

CPP payments can include a retirement pension as well as disability payments. OAS payments can include the OAS pension as well as the Guaranteed Income Supplement payments.

Notify property insurance companies

Notify property insurance companies of the death to ensure ongoing and adequate coverage of the house and other real estate, for protection in the event of an accident or fire. You should also lock and secure any vehicles to prevent use and confirm that adequate insurance is in place.

Notify life insurance companies

The life insurance companies need to be contacted so that they can begin processing any claim. See chapter five. They will need to be provided with a copy of the death certificate and the contact details of the life insurance beneficiaries.

Terminate lease

If the deceased was renting an apartment, or was a resident in a nursing home, arrange to store their possessions and cancel the lease. If there was a fixed term lease, then the landlord will have a legal obligation to mitigate by taking reasonable steps to try and rent it once the deceased's property has been removed.

As you go through the deceased's personal items, add those items to the list of assets below.

Make a list of assets and liabilities

Make a list of assets, with their "opening" values as of the date of death. You have an obligation to keep a complete accounting for all assets (see chapter thirteen). Also, to file the personal income tax return, income tax returns for the estate, and the estate administration tax return, you will need the value of each asset as at the date of death. For personal possessions, it is not necessary to record each item, but it would be helpful to keep a list so that you can record how personal items are distributed.

Make a list of liabilities

You are responsible for the payment by the estate of all of the deceased's and the estate's debts and income taxes, to the extent that there are sufficient funds in the estate. If you know that there are sufficient assets to pay all of the debts and taxes, then you should pay those debts which incur the highest interest rate charges first, such as credit cards.

You should review the deceased's banking records for the last few months to confirm that there were no suspicious charges or withdrawals.

Traditionally, estate lawyers have recommended the advertisement for creditors in the local newspaper. This is to establish that you have made reasonable efforts to locate legitimate creditors. As society changes, and fewer people read traditional newspapers, other efforts should be considered. For example, the deceased's personal papers, paid invoices, contracts, and work records should be reviewed to see if any potential creditors should be notified. Whether or not to advertise for creditors and how to do so, should be discussed with your estate lawyer.

For accounting purposes, we recommend a spreadsheet in Excel or Google Sheets, with separate sheets for each asset. This spreadsheet will allow you to begin recording the accounts as described in chapter thirteen. This example spreadsheet is available for free on the Allen & Allen website:

www.allenandallen.ca/the-estate-accounting-sample

See next page

Assets	Account number	Opening
Chequing account	01-xxxxx	1,500.00
Savings account	02-xxxxx	7,500.00
RRSP account	03-xxxxx	75,000.00
TFSA account	04-xxxxx	50,000.00
Investment account	05-xxxxx	125,000.00
Home	06-xxxxx	750,000.00
Art and paintings	08-xxxxx	1,500.00
Jewelry	09-xxxxx	1,000.00
Car	10-xxxxx	6,000.00
Liabilities		
Line of credit	11-xxxxx	(25,000.00)
Credit card	12-xxxxx	(5,000.00)
Total		987,500.00

Contact financial institutions

Arrange for a meeting with the deceased's bank(s). Once the bank receives proof of death, it should create an estate account and transfer all bank accounts held solely in the deceased's name into the estate account. It may require a notarized copy of the will and death certificate to do so. If there are any accounts which are registered in the deceased's name and another as joint owners, then the joint account will not be transferred into the estate account; instead, the surviving joint owner will be entitled to deal with those funds. You should make a note of any accounts in joint names so that you can determine later whether the funds are to be held for the estate, either by virtue of a declaration to that effect or by a resulting trust (see chapter seven).

You should direct the financial institution to convert the investment accounts into secure investments, such as GICs or cash equivalent. Sometimes, an investment advisor may be reluctant to change the investment portfolio, since the advisor may be earning higher commissions with growth-oriented investments which carry more risk. Unless all of the beneficiaries instruct you otherwise, the investments should be converted. Your role is to preserve assets and transfer the remainder of the estate to the beneficiaries as soon as practicable. If you retain speculative investments and the stock market crashes, you could be liable for breaching your "duty to take reasonable care" as described in chapter two.

Chapter Two—Duties and Powers of the Estate Trustee

What are your duties and powers as estate trustee?

Is an estate a trust?

An estate is arguably not a trust, even though you are appointed the estate *trustee*. Your role is closer to liquidator, required by law to pay the debts and taxes, and then to distribute as set out in the will (or by the laws of intestacy if there is no will) as soon as reasonably possible. Once the debts and taxes are paid, then the estate effectively does become a trust for the beneficiaries. Sometimes, the estate trustee is required to transfer assets to an ongoing "testamentary trust" which can last for many years, such as a spousal or children's trust.

You have a duty of loyalty, fairness, and a duty to take reasonable care.

Duty of loyalty

You must put the interests of the beneficiaries first. This is unlike parties to a contract or the relationship of creditor and debtor, where parties can put their own interests first and there is no duty to others, except for some basic rules of fair play. The interests of parties to a contract or the interests of the creditor can conflict, but a trustee is to avoid any conflict with the interests of the beneficiaries.

What happens if you are also one of the beneficiaries (*e.g.* one of the deceased's three children)? Must you favour the other two children? The answer is no, but you must treat all the beneficiaries, including yourself, fairly and equitably. If there is any transaction that might appear to favour you, then you should provide your siblings full disclosure and seek their written consent before proceeding. If your siblings do not consent and you wish to proceed, then apply to the Superior Court for approval with full disclosure of the conflict and the values of any relevant property.

What kinds of transactions create a conflict? Suppose you wish to buy the family cottage from the estate, or an interest in the deceased's private business. An option to do this may be included in the will, but the question of course becomes at what price and on what terms? Clearly, there is a conflict of interest. The solution is to obtain a market valuation from an independent professional appraiser and seek the written consent of the other beneficiaries or, if the beneficiaries refuse, court approval.

The fiduciary duty of loyalty is your personal obligation and you cannot delegate it to another. You can delegate administrative functions, such as filing income tax returns and preparing legal documents, but you must maintain oversight and you must make the important decisions.

Duty of fairness

You have a duty of fairness to all potential beneficiaries. Suppose the will sets up a spousal trust, with "income to my spouse until she dies, then divide the remainder equally among my children who are alive at that time." You must choose a portfolio of investments that does not favour the spouse's need to maximize income during her lifetime (such as preferred shares which pay high dividends) or the children's desire to maximize the appreciation of capital (such as common shares which pay no dividends but which increase in value over time.)

If, however, the will specifies the property that you are to retain, then the requirement to convert to a more balanced portfolio may be lessened. It would depend on the intentions expressed in the will and the fairness of the situation.

Duty to take reasonable care

You must exercise reasonable care in the administration of the estate. Failure to do so will give the beneficiaries (and creditors if they have not been paid) a claim in negligence and breach of trust. Various remedies would be available, including (but not limited to) the following:

- Setting aside a sale, unless it was sold to a *bona fide* purchaser for value without notice of the breach of trust;
- Replacing you as the estate trustee;
- Cancelling your compensation;
- Awarding legal costs against you;
- Adjusting the beneficial rights under the will; or
- Paying any profit you received back to the estate.

Joint liability for all estate trustees

Unless the will states otherwise, all estate trustees are responsible for all decisions, and all are liable for the negligence or breach of trust of one. However, if one estate trustee commits the wrongdoing, the innocent estate trustee can seek reimbursement from the wrongdoing estate trustee for any damages the innocent estate trustee is expected to pay.

Intermingling of assets

You should not combine any assets being held for the estate with your personal assets. This may seem obvious for organizational and accounting reasons, but it is also important to protect the estate assets in case you become sued for a matter unrelated to the estate and a third party takes steps to seize your personal assets.

Delegating administrative functions

You may be administering an estate for the first time (probably for a friend or for a family member), so you would not be expected to know, without professional advice, how to complete the more complicated legal, financial, tax, and accounting tasks. You can retain professionals, such as lawyers, accountants, investment advisors, and real estate valuators. The reasonable fees charged by these professionals are to be paid out of the estate and, generally, do not reduce your compensation.

If the professional assumes responsibility for preparing the estate accounts for the beneficiaries, however, the fees charged by the professional should be deducted from any compensation you claim as estate trustee (see chapter fourteen.) Preparing accounts for the beneficiaries is part of the responsibility that you are being compensated for, so to separately pay the professional's fees would be double counting for the same service and unfair to the beneficiaries.

Trustee powers that cannot be delegated

Some of your decisions cannot be delegated. For example, how to keep an even hand between the income and capital beneficiaries of a trust, is your decision. Similarly, the decision to sell estate assets and what general terms are appropriate is your decision, not the professionals.

Often in trusts, there is power to the trustee to access income and capital for a beneficiary if needed. For example, the following is a typical clause in a grandchild's trust:

> "If a grandchild of mine is to receive part of my estate and is under the age of majority, hold that part in a trust fund and pay the balance of the fund to the grandchild when she or he reaches majority. Before then, from time to time as you decide, you, my estate trustee, may pay all, part or none of the income and capital of the fund to the grandchild or for her or his benefit."

The decision to use all, part or none of the income and capital of the fund to, or for the benefit of, the grandchild is for you to make and cannot be delegated. You should keep detailed notes of your decisions, with explanations about why they were made. As long as there is a reasonable basis for your decision, the court should not second-guess it (otherwise, the court would effectively be appointing itself as trustee, contrary to the wishes of the will-maker.)

Investments for ongoing trusts

If you are to hold part of the estate in an ongoing trust, such as a spousal or children's trust, then you should diversify the investments according to general economic and market conditions, and you must consider the following criteria:

- the possible effect of inflation or deflation;
- the expected income tax consequences of investment decisions or strategies;
- the role that each investment or course of action plays within the overall trust portfolio;
- the expected total return from income and the appreciation of capital;
- the need for liquidity, regularity of income and preservation or appreciation of capital; and
- an asset's special relationship or special value, if any, to the purposes of the trust or to one or more of the beneficiaries.[1]

In making these decisions, you may not only rely on professional advice but also authorize an agent to exercise any of your investment powers, to the extent that a prudent investor would. However, you must first have a written plan or strategy, agreed to in writing by the agent, comprising reasonable assessments of risk and return, to be reported to you at regular stated intervals, and to be monitored by you.[2]

---

[1] *Trustee Act,* R.S.O. 1990, c. T.23 s 27.
[2] *Ibid,* s. 27.1.

Chapter Three—Jurisdiction of the Estate

Today, people move frequently, between provinces, between countries, temporarily and permanently, and sometimes their properties and investments follow their path, like breadcrumbs. In which province or country should you file for probate (see chapter four), which legal system applies to the validity and interpretation of the will, which legal system governs spousal and dependant support rights, and where should you file income tax returns?

Private international law—the basics

Private international law has conventions adopted by many legal systems which recognize the laws, and sometimes the authority of, a foreign jurisdiction. In Ontario estate matters, to avoid a conflict of laws, the legal system that applies to the property is as follows:[1]

> For real estate ("immovable property") the law of where the land is located governs the legal rights, including estate succession matters, and including a surviving spouse's and children's rights to the real estate.
>
> For all other property ("movable property") the succession laws that govern are the laws of where the deceased was domiciled when she or he died. The property rights of spouses arising out of the marital relationship, however, are governed by the internal law of the place where both spouses had their last common habitual residence or, if there is no

---

[1] See *Succession Law Reform Act*, R.S.O. 1990, c. S.26, ss 34-41; and *Family Law Act*, R.S.O. 1990, c. F.3, s 15.

place where the spouses had a common habitual residence, by the law of Ontario.

Domicile

Ontario law evolved from English common law, which developed the principle of "domicile." During the era of the British Empire, many English people emigrated to the colonies, where they raised their families, but they wanted their estate to be regulated by the "Home Country," where they kept their social roots and where they expected to return some day. Thus, to the extent possible, the laws that applied to their estate, no matter where they resided on death, remained the estate laws of England.

A child's "domicile of origin" is the permanent home of their parent(s) at the time when the child was born. Later, an adult may acquire a "domicile of choice" by taking up residence in a different province or country with the intention of continuing to reside there indefinitely. A person acquires a new domicile only when they have a fixed intention of establishing a permanent residence and this intention has been carried out by actual residence there.[2] Domicile is not necessarily the same as current residence or nationality.

Validity of the will

By section 37 of Ontario's *Succession Law Reform Act*, the *formalities of making the will* (for an interest in land or movables) are valid, if, when the will was signed, it complied with the internal law of (a) where the will was signed, (b) where the will-maker was then

---

[2] Castel & Walker, *Canadian Conflict of Laws*, 6th Edition (Toronto: LexisNexis, 2005), at s. 4.7

domiciled, (c) where the will-maker had their habitual residence, or (d) if the will-maker was a national, that nation's law governing the wills of nationals. In other words, as long as the will is signed in accordance with the rules of one of these places, then the will is a valid document in Ontario and would be accepted by the Ontario court for probate.

The *essential validity and effect* of the will, so far as it relates to an interest in land, is governed by the internal law of the place where the land is situated and the *essential validity and effect* of the will, so far as it relates to an interest in movables, is governed by the internal law of the place where the will-maker was domiciled at the time of death (see section 36 of the *Succession Law Reform Act*). This means that the law of where the will-maker was domiciled generally decides the interpretation of the clauses in the will and how property is to be distributed, along with the rules regarding capacity, undue influence, public policy, and the other litigation issues (see chapter seven), except for real estate, which would be decided according to the law of where the land is located.

Jurisdiction can become complicated. For example, what if the deceased ("Sophia") was born in Quebec, had been working in England for a year, signed her will in England, died tragically during a vacation in Spain, her principal residence is in Toronto, she owns an investment condominium in Florida, and most of her financial investments are listed on the New York Stock Exchange? In which jurisdiction should the estate trustee file for probate, and which legal system would apply to the validity and interpretation of her will?

The Ontario Court would probate and accept the formal validity of Sophia's will if it is valid according to English law (where she signed it) or Ontario law, where she was domiciled. Ontario law would decide the interpretation and the essential validity of her will for all her assets, except her Florida condominium. This is because Ontario was her domicile and the location of her Toronto home. Florida law would decide the application of her will regarding her Florida condominium, where the land is located. Even though Ontario law would apply to most of her assets, her estate trustee may need to probate her will in New York and Florida, to prove the authority of her will to the institutions in those jurisdictions. To do so, her estate trustee would first obtain probate in Ontario, and then "republish" the will in the foreign jurisdiction through a process called resealing.

How does an Ontario court apply foreign law? The court would rely on the opinion of a law expert who would testify about what the laws of the foreign jurisdiction are.

Income tax returns

Individuals file income tax returns in Canada if they are a Canadian resident, based on their worldwide income received. This is different from US rules, which requires all American citizens to file US tax returns based on their worldwide income, regardless of where they reside. Canada has income tax treaties with many nations, so that a category of income taxes paid in one jurisdiction will likely be reduced by the same category of income taxes paid in the other jurisdiction by the provisions of the *Income Tax Act* and the respective tax treaty.

If Sophia was considered a permanent resident of England at her date of death, her estate trustee would not need to file a Canadian income tax return. If, however, she was considered for income tax purposes to be a visitor to England, the estate trustee would need to file a Canadian income tax return based on her worldwide income and could seek a credit for any English income tax payments made. She may also have had income tax deducted from her US investment income earned, which the estate trustee would want to claim as a foreign tax credit against her Canadian income tax payable.

Chapter Four—Getting Probate

A Certificate of Appointment of Estate Trustee (formerly known as "probate") is a document issued by the Ontario Superior Court stating that the person named in the certificate is the estate trustee and is authorized to deal with the estate assets.

A Certificate of Appointment of Estate Trustee with a Will attaches a copy of the will. If there is no valid will, a Certificate of Appointment of Estate Trustee Without a Will is issued. See chapter eleven. There are other kinds of court certificates as noted below.

Will the estate trustee need a Certificate of Appointment?

If there is a valid will, your authority is derived from the will immediately following death, whether or not the court later certifies it. Whether you need a Certificate of Appointment (and whether the Estate Administration Tax is payable) is determined by which institutions control the record of title to the deceased's assets and what degree of proof they require to record a change of ownership. Section 49 of the Ontario *Evidence Act* provides that a Certificate of Appointment is, in the absence of evidence to the contrary, proof of the validity and contents of the will.

If the deceased owned real estate registered in the Land Titles system (in which most Ontario properties are now registered), the Land Titles Registrar will normally require a Certificate of Appointment to record your authority to deal with the land. Some properties are still in the old land Registry system, which does not require a Certificate of Appointment to transfer good title; other properties, which have been converted to Land Titles from land Registry, allow for a "first dealing" with the land without a Certificate of Appointment, provided that certain statements and indemnities are provided to the Land Titles Registrar. See chapter five.

You will usually need a Certificate of Appointment before you are given access to the deceased's significant bank accounts and publicly traded securities registered solely in the deceased's name. This is because the institutions holding the assets do not wish to assume the risk that the will presented is not the last and valid will of the deceased. In some cases, however, where the proceeds in the account are not large, and where suitable indemnities can be provided, the institution may waive the requirement for a Certificate of Appointment.

Note: A debtor can insist that you obtain a Certificate of Appointment to confirm that you are authorized to discharge the debt on payment.

Assets that do not require a Certificate of Appointment to be administered

Many institutions or recipients will not require a Certificate of Appointment to transfer assets. For example:

- Assets jointly held with someone who survives. The survivor can register title ownership ("survivorship") on filing a notarial copy of the death certificate.

- Assets that pass directly to a designated beneficiary and not to the deceased's estate. These may include life insurance proceeds and funds from a registered retirement saving plan

(RRSP), a registered retirement income fund (RRIF), or a tax-free savings account (TFSA).

- Shares of a private corporation: The surviving directors of a private corporation do not need a Certificate of Appointment to transfer title to the deceased's shares in the corporation to the survivor(s).[1]

- Personal and household effects: Usually, no Certificate of Appointment is required to transfer ownership.

- Automobiles: The Ontario Ministry of Transportation does not require a Certificate of Appointment to transfer vehicle ownership, but it will require a notarial copy of the will and a statutory declaration.

The Estate Administration Tax

When you file for a Certificate of Appointment, you must pay the Estate Administration Tax. The tax is about 1.5% of the estate's gross value less real estate encumbrances.[2] If you need a Certificate of Appointment for some estate assets, the tax is calculated on the value of *all* of the assets being administered by the will or by the intestacy (less real estate encumbrances), not just those assets requiring a Certificate of Appointment to be administered. (Jointly

---

[1] *Business Corporations Act,* R.S.O. 1990, c.B.16, s.67(8)

[2] As of January 1, 2020, Ontario eliminated the estate administration tax on estates valued under $50,000. The tax is $15 for each $1,000 or part thereof by which the value of the estate exceeds $50,000. See *Estate Administration Tax Act*, 1998, S.O. 1998, c. 34, Sched., s 2(6.1).

owned assets are excluded because they go to the surviving joint owner directly and not through the deceased's will.)

The tax can be significant because it is based on the gross value of assets rather than the gain in their values. On an estate of $1 million (including equity in the family home), the estate administration tax is about $15,000 plus legal costs to obtain the certificate. Also, in many regions of Ontario, there are bureaucratic delays in having the application for a Certificate of Appointment processed by court staff.

If the deceased had more than one will, then in some cases the "secondary will" can be used for the non-probate assets and the "primary will" is filed with the court for those assets which require a Certificate of Appointment to be administered.

Within 180 days of the Certificate of Appointment being issued, you must file an "Estate Information Return" with the Ontario Ministry of Finance disclosing the details and values at death of all the assets flowing through the will filed with the court. If, at a later date, additional assets or more accurate values are determined, then you will have sixty days to file an amended return and pay the additional tax (or seek a refund of tax) based on the amended values.

Be careful that the information in the Estate Information Return is correct. If your fail to provide accurate information, you may face fines of up to twice the amount of tax owing and even imprisonment. You can defend yourself by showing that you took reasonable steps to determine the tax owing. Unlike the *Income Tax Act*, you cannot obtain a clearance certificate from the Ministry of Finance to certify that the Ministry accepts that the Estate Information Return was properly filed.

How to obtain a Certificate of Appointment

The application is normally handled by a lawyer. The process under Rule 74.04 of the Ontario *Rules of Civil Procedure* requires the filing of an application to court sworn by the estate trustee and disclosing the value of the assets, the original will, proof of death, an affidavit attesting that a notice of application has been served on all of the beneficiaries, an affidavit from the witness to the signing of the will, and, in some cases, other documents.

Before filing, you must serve by regular mail notice of the application on all persons entitled to share in the distribution of the estate, including contingent beneficiaries. Attached to this notice is a copy of the will, but you are not required to serve a copy of the entire will on a beneficiary who receives specified cash or a gift of a specified item, just the relevant portion of the will. If a beneficiary is a minor, the beneficiary's parent or guardian and the Office of the Children's Lawyer is to be served. If a beneficiary is mentally incompetent, the beneficiary's guardian or attorney for property or the Public Guardian and Trustee is to be served.

If you are appointed estate trustee and you reside outside of the Commonwealth, you must post an administration bond with the court, at twice the estimated value of the estate. This can be dispensed with if adequate evidence is presented to the court that you have a good financial record, that there are more than enough assets in Ontario for any creditors and dependants of the estate, that the beneficiaries are all adults, mentally capable, and have all consented in writing.

If there is no will, then your application to the court is similar and an administration bond is required. You must be a resident of Ontario. As mentioned in chapter eleven, an application can be made to dispense with the bond, which is usually granted if the estate trustee has a good financial record, there are more than enough assets in the estate for any creditors and dependants, the beneficiaries are all adults, mentally capable, and have all consented in writing.

Estate trustee renouncing an appointment

Just because you are named in the will as the estate trustee does not mean that you must accept the appointment. You can renounce by filing form 74.11 with the Estates Court if you have not started to administer the estate or applied for a Certificate of Appointment. If you have already done so, you must apply under subsection 37(1) of the *Trustee Act* to the Superior Court for a Removal Order. If the Court approves this, you can still be liable for your acts or omissions as estate trustee. As such, you should provide the beneficiaries with your accounts and get them to sign releases. If they refuse, you may need the Court's approval of your accounts.

Removal of an estate trustee

Any person with a financial interest in an estate can apply to the Ontario Superior Court to remove the estate trustee. The court will remove the estate trustee only if the applicant shows that it is necessary to do so on a balance of probabilities because the estate trustee is unlikely to administer the estate properly with due regard to the welfare of the beneficiaries. Examples include where the estate trustee becomes mentally incapable, is dishonest or endangers the estate assets, there is a disagreement among the estate trustees which cannot be resolved, or there is a conflict of interest which cannot be resolved.

Successor estate trustee

If an estate trustee dies while the estate is being administered, becomes incapable of acting, or is removed by the court, a successor estate trustee is appointed. The appointment process is similar to the process for appointing the first estate trustee. The certificate to be issued is a "Certificate of Appointment of Succeeding Estate Trustee with a Will".

Appointment of Foreign Estate Nominee in Ontario

If probate has been obtained in a foreign jurisdiction, and if there are assets in Ontario that need an estate trustee appointed in Ontario to be administered, then the process of appointing a nominee in Ontario involves filing a certified copy of the foreign probate, sealed by the foreign court, with a nomination process for the Ontario estate trustee. An administration bond is required, unless the court grants an exception.

Estate Trustee During Litigation

If the named estate trustee is in a conflict of interest and there is litigation involving the estate, then the court will appoint a neutral person to administer the estate during the litigation period. For example, if the spouse is named as estate trustee in the will and the spouse is also suing the estate for property equalization and/or support, then a different person should be appointed Estate Trustee

During Litigation until such time as the litigation is settled or determined.

Chapter Five—Collecting and Preserving the Assets

From chapter one, you will have started to collect and preserve the estate assets to ensure that all of the estate liabilities will be paid and that any remaining assets will be distributed in accordance with the terms of the will, or by the laws of intestacy if there is no will. You must account for all assets. See chapter thirteen. Also, to file the income tax returns and the estate administration (probate) tax return, you will need to record the asset values as of the date of death.

Personal items

If the deceased left personal items to be divided among a group of beneficiaries, rather than just to one beneficiary, you should preserve and list those items. These items can include jewelry, clothing, books, paintings, and art objects. Sometimes, the will gives the estate trustee the power to choose how to distribute personal items among the will-maker's family and friends. Personal items can trigger emotional attachments, and so, to the extent possible, it is important to achieve harmony, or at least a sense of fairness, when distributing personal items. One strategy is to circulate the list of items and confidentially ask the beneficiaries which items they would like to receive and in which priority. Another strategy for a family distribution is to give each sibling a pecking order (perhaps in order of age) to take turns choosing personal items.

For any jewelry or potentially valuable assets, you should have them appraised by a professional jeweller or valuator. This is for income tax and estate administration tax purposes and to assist you in determining the fairness of distributions among the beneficiaries.

Digital assets

It is likely that the estate you are administering has "digital assets," which include files stored on digital devices, along with email, web hosting, and social network accounts. Some lawyers recommend that specific reference is made in the will for the transfer of digital assets, but this is not common. More important is to gain access to the deceased's accounts and passwords. This will allow you to cancel any online accounts and subscriptions. Also, it may allow you to post a memorial for the deceased on social media accounts.

Life insurance

Determine if the deceased had life insurance and whether a designated beneficiary is listed in the policy. If there is a designated beneficiary, the insurance proceeds go directly to the beneficiary and do not form part of the estate (unless the designated beneficiary holds the proceeds in trust for the estate. See chapter seven.)

An advantage of having a designated beneficiary of a life insurance policy, whether it be the spouse or someone else, is that the proceeds normally do not flow into the estate and become included in the calculation of the Estate Administration Tax. Also, as discussed in chapter six, the life insurance proceeds could be protected from creditors if the estate is bankrupt. However, if there is a dependant support claim against the estate, the insurance proceeds can be seized and included in the assets for support, so it is important to record the amount of the payout and to whom.

Pensions

If the deceased had a pension, their spouse (including a common law spouse of at least three years duration) is entitled to receive the benefit of that pension even if a different beneficiary is named, unless the spouses were living separate and apart.[1] The surviving spouse will either collect periodic payments or a lump sum payout. Any lump-sum payout of the deceased's pension can generally be transferred tax-free to a surviving spouse's RRSP or RRIF. If the beneficiary is not a spouse, then the beneficiary pays income tax on the payout, and if there is no beneficiary named, it becomes payable to the estate and the estate pays income tax on the payout.

Canada Pension Plan (CPP)

A survivor's CPP pension is available to the spouse, and a children's benefit for any dependant children. If there is no surviving spouse or dependant children, you can claim a $2,500 death benefit for the estate. To be eligible, the deceased must have made contributions to the CPP for a minimum number of years. To apply, complete the "Application for a Canada Pension Plan Death Benefit" (ISP1200) and include a certified true copy of the death certificate, then mail it to the closest Service Canada Centre. You can find the address by calling Service Canada at 1-800-622-6232. Apply for the benefit within 60 days of the date of death.

---

[1] *Pension Benefit Act,* R.S.O. 1990, c.P.8

Real estate

If the deceased owned a house, condominium, cottage, or investment property, you need to know how the title is registered.

Most land in Ontario is registered in the Land Titles system, having evolved from the old land Registry system. Under the Registry system, title to land could be transferred without probate, but under Land Titles, probate is required if land passes through an estate, with some exceptions.

Title to land can be registered in several ways, the most common of which are these:

1. "Registered owner"—If the deceased was the sole registered owner, probate will be required in Land Titles to confirm your authority to transfer title. An application to transfer title to the estate trustee is first registered, and then you can either sell the property or distribute it to the beneficiaries, depending on the wording of the will.

   There are some exceptions. You can transfer title without probate if the total value of the estate is less than $50,000. There is a "first dealings" exemption where the deceased acquired the property while it was registered under the Registry System and continued to be registered on title, uninterrupted, after it was converted to Land Titles. Also, there is a process for real estate that is not transferred to the estate trustee within three years to become vested in the beneficiaries directly without a Certificate of Appointment of Estate Trustee.

If one of these exceptions could apply, you should speak with a lawyer.

2. "Joint Tenants"—If the deceased was registered along with another, perhaps the deceased's spouse or adult child, as joint tenants, the surviving joint tenant will automatically be entitled to be recorded as the 100% owner. All that is needed is a death certificate.

3. "Tenants in Common"—Each owner owns a percentage of the property. If the percentage is not stated, they will be presumed to own an equal percentage. When one tenant dies, that person's percentage passes through their estate in the same manner as a registered owner's interest passes through their estate, as in #1 above. Thus, you may need probate to transfer title for an interest in Land Titles owned by a tenant in common.

4. "Life interest" and "remainder interest"—although uncommon in Ontario, it is possible to have one person as the 100% owner during their lifetime, and when they die, the "remainderman" is entitled to 100% ownership. All that is needed is a death certificate.

5. Corporate ownership—a corporation is considered in law to be a separate legal person. Thus, a corporation can be recorded as the legal owner of real estate. If the deceased is the sole shareholder of the corporation, these details are not recorded on title, and the corporation continues to exist, will remain the owner, and can deal with the property after the shareholder's death. You, as the estate trustee, will become

the owner of the deceased's shares of the corporation and can appoint directors of the corporation to transfer the real estate in accordance with the deceased's will without probate.

What about ownership in a trust? The Registry system allowed for the recording of trusts on title, but Land Titles does not. A trust is not a legal person, but an obligation on a legal owner to the beneficiaries. Land Titles only records who the legal owner is and does not concern itself with trust obligations which may be imposed on the legal owner.

Assemble whatever real estate documents you have and ask a lawyer to search title to confirm how title is currently held. That way, you will know whether probate is required and whether there are any mortgages or liens registered against the property (mortgages reduce the amount of the probate tax). You should also determine whether the property taxes have been paid in full.

You should locate documents to determine the value of the property when it was purchased, the value when the deceased died, and its current value. You must do this for the following reasons:

- You need to know the value of the property when it was purchased to calculate the capital gain for income tax purposes. A capital gain on a principal residence may be fully or partially exempt from income tax, but the capital gain on other real estate is likely fully taxable. You need to know the purchase price to calculate the "Adjusted Cost Base" (i.e. tax cost), as well as any costs spent in acquiring or improving the property. The higher the Adjusted Cost Base, the lower the capital gain and the lower the income tax.

- You need to know the value of the property on death to determine the "deemed disposition" value. The *Income Tax Act* deems it as though a person sells all of their property at fair market value on their death, and the capital gain is included in their final income tax return unless the property is given to the spouse (see chapter eight). You also need the values of all property flowing through the will on death to calculate the Estate Administration (probate) Tax. If the real estate is not sold to an arm's length purchaser soon after death, then, for the at-death value, you should decide whether you will either rely on the MPAC value or obtain a professional valuation. The latter is more accurate, and it is important to be accurate because you will be personally responsible for the income tax on the capital gain.

- You need to know the current value of the property if the estate retained it for a few years after the deceased's death, perhaps because it is part of a continuing trust, or you and the beneficiaries agreed to retain the property. For example, sometimes the beneficiaries may wish to enjoy the family cottage for a few years before selling it. In these cases, there could be an increase in value after death, and so the estate will have to calculate the capital gain on that increase and be subject to income tax on the sale.

Review the will to determine if any of the beneficiaries have the right to use the property for a period, or to inherit the property specifically.

Determine if the surviving spouse has a claim for possession of the "matrimonial home." There can be more than one matrimonial home: the traditional home, a summer cottage, ski chalet, timeshare unit for vacations, etc. "Matrimonial home" is defined in the Ontario *Family Law Act* as "every property in which a person has an interest and that is or, if the spouses have separated, was at the time of separation ordinarily occupied by the person and his or her spouse as their family residence."[2] A spouse who has no interest in a matrimonial home but is occupying it at the time of the other spouse's death, whether under an order for exclusive possession or otherwise, is entitled to retain possession for sixty days after the spouse's death against the spouse's estate rent free.[3]

If the property is sold, consider having your lawyer retain the sale proceeds in a solicitor's trust account rather than immediately transferring the proceeds to the estate account, for the reasons discussed below.

Probate and the "estate account"

If you can sell the property without probate because of one of the exceptions noted above, do not necessarily transfer the proceeds to the estate account, because you will need probate to release those funds. Instead, if probate can be avoided, ask the real estate lawyer to hold the funds in trust.

---

[2] *Family Law Act*, R.S.O. 1990, c. F.3, s 18.
[3] *Ibid,* s 26(2).

You will likely need probate to access large bank accounts that are solely in the name of the deceased. Banks and financial institutions are not legally required to demand probate, but they generally do if the value in an account exceeds about $25,000 (the amount is in the bank's discretion.) Banks and financial institutions avoid risk. One can imagine a situation where the bank releases funds to an estate trustee noted in a will presented to the bank, and later, another person claims to be the estate trustee and presents a more recent will of the deceased. Banks prefer probate because section 49 of the *Evidence Act* (Ontario) provides that a court certificate is, in the absence of evidence to the contrary, proof of the validity and contents of the will. For a more detailed explanation regarding probate, see chapter four.

Investments (non-registered)

This discussion is for "non-registered" investments. Non-registered investments include stocks, bonds, and/or mutual funds. (A "registered" investment is registered with the Canada Revenue Agency for income tax deferral purposes, such as RRSPs, RRIFs, DPSPs, and RPPs, or for no income tax at all, as with TFSAs. See below.)

If the deceased owned non-registered investments, determine how title is recorded to the accounts. If the deceased was the sole owner of an investment account, the financial institution that controls the account will probably require probate. If the account was jointly held with another person, such as the deceased's spouse or adult child, then the survivor will automatically be entitled to be recorded as the legal owner. However, you need to determine if the surviving owner (particularly if the surviving owner is the deceased's child) is holding some or all the account in trust for the estate. See chapter seven and the discussions of "resulting trust" and "dependant support."

Determine (i) the value of each security within the portfolio when it was purchased by the deceased, (ii) their values when the deceased died, and (iii) their current values. The deceased's investment advisor can assemble these values for you quite easily.

RRSPs and RRIFs

A registered retirement savings plan (RRSP) and a registered retirement income fund (RRIF) are accounts in which income tax is not payable until funds are withdrawn. Contributions into an RRSP are tax deductible (up to a maximum contribution limit), and then, when the RRSP or RRIF funds are withdrawn they are taxable. On death, these plans are considered to be *de-registered* resulting in all of their value to be taxable. However, there is a tax-free transfer available to the surviving spouse's RRSP or RRIF, and there is an opportunity to reduce the tax where RRSP and RRIF funds are transferred to a financially dependent child or grandchild. See the discussion in chapter eight.

RRSPs and RRIFs allow the owner to designate someone else to receive the proceeds on their death. Because of the tax-free transfer available, it is normally wise to designate one's spouse as the recipient. The income tax won't be payable until the earlier of when the surviving spouse withdraws from their RRSP or RRIF or the surviving spouse's death. If the estate receives the proceeds, it can elect with the surviving spouse to transfer it directly to the spouse's RRSP or RRIF. Thus, it is wise to speak to a tax specialist before allowing funds that could have gone to the spouse to be paid into the estate.

An advantage of having a designated beneficiary of a RRSP or RRIF, whether it be the spouse or someone else, is that the proceeds normally do not flow into the estate and become included in the calculation of the probate tax. Also, as discussed in chapter six, the proceeds of the RRSP or RRIF could be protected from general creditors in the event that the estate is bankrupt. However, at the time of writing, there is a recent Ontario case which has held that the designated recipient of an RRSP or RRIF holds those funds for the estate on a resulting trust, unless there is an expressed intention otherwise.[4] Also, if there is a dependant support claim against the estate, the RRSP or RRIF can be seized and included in the assets for support, so it is important to record the amount of the payout and to whom. See chapter seven.

If the RRSP or RRIF goes directly to a beneficiary who is not the surviving spouse or a dependant child, then the total value of the RRSP or RRIF is included in the deceased's final personal income tax return. See chapter eight. Thus, it is effectively the estate which pays the income tax. If the beneficiary of the plan is the same person as the beneficiary of the estate, then there is no unfairness. The beneficiary of the plan is liable to pay the income tax if the estate is bankrupt.

---

[4] *Calmusky v. Calmusky*, 2020 ONSC 1506

Tax Free Savings Account (TFSA)

Unlike an RRSP, there is no tax deduction for contributing funds into a TFSA; accordingly, there is no income tax when funds are withdrawn from a TFSA. The benefit of a TFSA is that, while funds are held in the account, it does not accumulate income tax.
You should determine whether the TFSA has a beneficiary or a successor holder. The successor holder must be a spouse or common-law partner. A beneficiary of a TFSA can be the spouse, the deceased's children, a third party, or a registered charity. If there is no beneficiary or a successor holder, the TFSA forms part of the estate.

Private corporations

Determine if the deceased was a shareholder of any private corporation, and if so, whether the corporation has other shareholders. What assets does the corporation own? What liabilities does it have? What contracts was the deceased subject to, such as a shareholders' or employment agreement? You need to know how the deceased's interest can be wound-up without incurring liabilities to the estate and in the most tax-efficient manner. Professional advice is recommended.

Trusts

Was the deceased a beneficiary of a trust, and if so, who are the other beneficiaries and who are the trustees? Or, was the deceased a trustee? Like private corporations, the varieties are numerous, and you should summarize the documents and seek professional advice.

Update your list of the assets

Update the values of the assets of the estate and input them into your accounting spreadsheet (see chapter thirteen). You should also have a sheet for assets that were designated directly to a beneficiary, so that you will know what amount can be returned to the estate in the event of a spousal or dependant support claim or if the funds are to be held on a resulting trust for the estate. See chapter seven.

Preserve assets

You should require the investment advisor to sell any speculative assets and convert all estate assets to cash or cash equivalent, such as a GIC, T-Bill, or "money market" mutual funds. See chapter one. Your job is to liquidate assets and transfer them to the beneficiaries. If, however, all the beneficiaries prefer that you keep the current portfolio, you should get their instructions in writing.

Chapter 6—Estate Liabilities

As the estate trustee, you are personally responsible for all the debts and liabilities of the estate, to the extent that the estate can pay them. If the estate is insolvent (i.e. if its liabilities exceed its assets now, and for the foreseeable future), then you are responsible only to the extent that the estate can pay the liabilities, and you can deduct from the estate reasonable compensation for your services. This is similar to the role of a trustee in bankruptcy. The trustee liquidates (sells) the assets for cash, and then distributes the cash by order of priority and then *pro rata* among the general creditors.

Typical liabilities of an estate

Some typical liabilities include mortgage payments, utility bills, funeral and burial expenses, income tax (see chapter eight) and estate administration tax (see chapter four).

Regular payments and subscriptions should be cancelled. It can be a chore to contact these service providers, because their customer relations are often atrocious. However, it is an important task to complete.

You should review the last few months of the deceased's bank accounts, to see if there were any unusual or suspicious transactions that need investigation.

Notifying creditors

A creditor who isn't aware of the death may not have sent a recent reminder to the deceased, and so it may be difficult for you to become aware of the debt. The deceased's record keeping may have become disorganized, especially if there was a long illness. It is important to take reasonable steps to locate any legitimate claims against the estate.

If you are unable to find all the creditors of the estate, you must provide potential creditors with notice. Pursuant to section 53 of the *Trustee Act*, after sending a notice to creditors (to expire after a reasonable period, usually 30 or 60 days), you may proceed to distribute the estate assets and will not be personally liable should there later be a claim from a creditor.

The *Trustee Act*, however, does not specify the manner of giving notice. Traditionally, estate trustees have advertised for creditors in the local newspaper, but this may not be appropriate because fewer people read local newspapers. What is reasonable notice to creditors will depend on the circumstances. Make sure to advertise for creditors in the area where the deceased was known to have resided or have had business dealings.

No court action can be taken for an unpaid account, debt, contract, or civil wrong against the estate, after two years from the date of death.[1] This is a "limitation period." In addition, there is a two-year limitation period from when the cause of action arose, which would likely expire even sooner.

---

[1] *Trustee Act*, R.S.O. 1990, c. T.23, s 38(3).

Family Law claims

As described in chapter seven, various family members can make claims against the estate:

- The surviving spouse has six months from the date of death to choose whether to share the increased net family property accumulated during the marriage or to receive under the will, or if there is no will, what is provided for by the intestacy. An application to extend the six-month limitation period is possible under section 1(8) of the *Family Law Act*.

- A dependant can make a claim for support under the *Succession Law Reform Act*. No application for support can be made after six months from the grant of a Certificate of Appointment of Estate Trustee. However, this can be extended under section 61(2) of the Act as to any portion of the estate remaining undistributed as at the date of the application.

- A spouse or partner, or any person for that matter, has up to two years from the date of death to assert a claim for a constructive trust against the deceased's estate. As noted in chapter seven, a constructive trust can arise if one person contributes to the value of another person's asset(s) without compensation. To remedy the "unjust enrichment," the court can declare that the legal owner holds the beneficial interest in trust for the contributor.

Insolvent estates

You must be cautious if the estate is insolvent. With an insolvent estate, you must distribute the net proceeds in the correct legal order and *pro rata* among the general creditors. If you are reluctant to assume these responsibilities, you can petition the estate into formal bankruptcy proceedings, and a trustee in bankruptcy will assume these responsibilities.

In an insolvent estate, you must pay debts in the following order:

- Reasonable and necessary funeral expenses;

- Testamentary expenses and costs to administer the estate, including payments to you, and the reasonable fees of professionals, such as the lawyer and accountant;

- Secured debts, which are debts held against a specific asset or a class of assets (e.g., mortgages on a house);

- Taxes (in Ontario it appears that federal income taxes receive priority over other unsecured debts);

- Debts with legislative priority, which may include child support, wages owed to employees, and employment insurance;

- Unsecured debts, which are all other debts owed by the estate (proportionately without any preference or priority).

The priority of which estate debts ought to be paid depends on whether the estate is administered as an insolvent estate (provincial law) or a bankrupt estate (federal law). For instance, the federal *Bankruptcy and Insolvency Act* provides that the payment of support arrears take priority over federal income taxes, but in the case of an insolvent estate, income taxes take priority.

One plan is for you to arrange the funeral, secure the assets, and then contact the creditors. You could negotiate to allow personal possessions to be distributed among the family, and then propose a methodology for the sale of assets, compensation for your services, and the distribution of assets *pro rata* among creditors (assuming no creditors have priority). If all the creditors approve, then you could undertake the responsibility. If one or more of the creditors objects, then you could choose to send the estate into formal bankruptcy proceedings.

Chapter 7—Litigation and the Estate

Litigation can be a nightmare—mostly unexpected, always unwanted, and usually too expensive. There is a perception that lawyers create litigation, but the truth is, that when a parent dies, rival children, an ex-spouse, troubled assets, or a history of family resentments, can explode like a powder keg. All the old grievances can surface, positions taken, things said, accusations made, and it will be your job as estate trustee to guide the family's ship through these troubled waters.

First question—are you in a conflict?

You have a duty to maximize the value of the estate, pay all of the legitimate debts, and deal with the beneficiaries fairly and as set out in the will, or by the laws of intestacy if there is no will.

If the settlement of any claim or the transfer or sale of any asset puts your personal interests in conflict with the estate's interest, you may need to resign as estate trustee. If so, the court will appoint a succeeding estate or an "Estate Trustee During Litigation." See chapter four.

Some conflicts are acceptable, however. The deceased may have anticipated them. For example, if the will states "divide my personal items among my children as you, my estate trustee, decide" and the deceased appointed his daughter as estate trustee, then the conflict was anticipated and she can give some of the personal items to herself, as long as she acts fairly to the others. Similarly, if the daughter was involved in the deceased's private company and his will gives her an option to purchase the deceased's shares in the company from his estate, the conflict was anticipated and she can remain estate trustee as she exercises her option and buys the shares. However, to do so, she should first obtain a valuation of the shares from an independent professional valuator and seek the consent of the other beneficiaries. If the other beneficiaries do not consent, she should seek the approval of the court for the transaction, though the court may not approve it. For example, when Steve Stavro was the executor of Harold Ballard's estate (the estate owned the Toronto Maple Leafs), Stavro acted for both the estate and the purchasers. Even though Stavro obtained two valuations, the court prevented the transaction and held that it was to be sold on the open market.[1]

Challenges to the validity of the will

As estate trustee, you have a duty to propound the will, i.e. put it forth as valid. Others may claim that the will is invalid; for example, that it did not reflect the deceased's intent when it was signed, because of mental capacity issues, or because the deceased was pressured or unduly influenced to sign.

You must prove that it was properly signed (usually with an "affidavit of execution") and that the deceased approved its contents and had the necessary mental capacity when it was signed. If the will was signed in accordance with the rules, the law presumes that the deceased knew and approved its contents and had the necessary capacity. However, if a challenger can show "suspicious circumstances," i.e. that the free will of the will-maker was overborne by acts of coercion, the burden of proof shifts back to the propounder of the will.

---

[1] *Ballard Estate (Re)*, 1994 CanLII 7305 (ON SC)

The following are potential indications of diminished capacity: The will-maker was elderly; had a mental disability; lacked control of their personal affairs; made strange dispositions; made drastic changes to their plan; or was unwilling to give their lawyer full information.

Even if the will-maker had capacity and knew and approved the contents of their will, it can still be challenged if it was obtained by influence amounting to coercion. The following are potential indications of undue influence: The will-maker became isolated; had recent family conflict; experienced recent bereavement; was emotionally or financially dependent on the beneficiary; made substantial pre-death transfers to the beneficiary; made statements of fearing the beneficiary; made a new will that was inconsistent with a prior will; failed to provide an explanation for leaving the entire estate to the beneficiary and excluding others who would be expected to inherit; the beneficiary selected the lawyer, who was previously unknown to the will-maker; the beneficiary conveyed the instructions to the lawyer; or the beneficiary received a draft of the will before it was signed and took the will-maker to the lawyer to have it signed.

Gifts which are void as against public policy

Some clauses in a will are void as against public policy. Historically, terms of a will are void if they impose i) conditions to induce celibacy or the separation of married couples; ii) conditions that undermine the parent-child relationship by disinheriting children if they live with a named parent; iii) conditions that disinherit beneficiaries if they change their membership in a designated church or religious faith; and iv) conditions that incite a beneficiary to commit a crime or do any act prohibited by law.[2]

If there is a clause in the deceased's will that is either contrary to these principles or contrary to the principles of the Ontario *Human Rights Code*, you should delay any distribution based on such a clause until you seek legal advice. Although the *Human Rights Code* does not apply to a gift or an inheritance, the court's interpretation of public policy evolves and would likely be informed by the principles of the *Human Rights Code*. For example, in 1990, the court voided the terms of a charitable trust created in 1923 which restricted educational scholarships to white Protestants.[3] If the will requires the estate trustee or a beneficiary to do something which is discriminatory or illegal, the clause may be void. However, the *motives* of the will-maker for including or excluding a person in their gift plan are generally not reviewable by the court.[4]

Family law property equalization claims

If the deceased left a surviving married spouse, you should refrain from any significant distributions for the first six months following the deceased's death.[5] During this time, the surviving spouse can choose to either receive under the will (or intestacy if there is no will) or share the increased net family property accumulated during the marriage.[6]

---

[2] *Spence v. BMO Trust Co.* 2016 Carswell Ont 3345, 2016 ONCA 196 [*Spence*] at para 55.

[3] *Canada Trust Co. v. Ontario* (Human Rights Commission) (1990), 69 D.L.R. (4th) 321, 12 C.H.R.R. D/184, 74 O.R. (2d) 481, 38 E.T.R. 1, (sub nom. Leonard Foundation Trust, Re) 37 O.A.C. 191, 1990 CarswellOnt 486 (Ont. C.A.)

[4] *Spence, supra* note 15.

[5] The spouse can apply to extend the limitation period beyond six months. See *Family Law Act*, R.S.O. 1990, c. F.3, s 1(8).

[6] *Ibid,* s. 6

The surviving married spouse must choose one or the other. If the survivor elects equalization, the will is interpreted as though the survivor had died first. Moreover, if the survivor receives benefits from the deceased's life insurance policies, a lump sum payment under a pension or similar plan of the deceased, or an entitlement by right of survivorship or otherwise on the death of the deceased spouse, including an RRSP or RRIF designated to the spouse,[7] the amount of such payment or value shall be credited against the surviving spouse's equalization claim (less any contingent tax liability in respect of such payment or receipt). If the net benefits exceed the equalization payment, the estate can demand the excess, unless there is a written designation by the deceased that the payments are to be in addition to equalization.[8]

A spouse must include and equalize the value of a matrimonial home owned at the end of the marriage but cannot deduct its value if it was owned at the beginning of the marriage. To some extent, the requirement to equally share the value of the matrimonial home can be reduced because debts related directly to the acquisition or significant improvement of a matrimonial home at the beginning are not deducted. There can be more than one matrimonial home: a summer cottage, ski chalet, timeshare unit for vacations, etc. In section 18 of the *Family Law Act*, "matrimonial home" is defined as "[e]very property in which a person has an interest and that is or, if the spouses have separated, was at the time of separation ordinarily occupied by the person and his or her spouse as their family residence."

---

[7] *Laframboise v. Laframboise* 2012 ONSC 4508, 2012 CarswellOnt 9719, [2013] W.D.F.L. 150, at para 20

[8] *Family Law Act, supra* note 18, s. 6(7).

If the court is of the opinion that equalizing the net family properties would be unconscionable, having regard to various circumstances, it may award a spouse an amount that is more or less than half the difference between the net family properties.

In case an equalization claim is made, you should not distribute more than a modest amount from the estate for six months following death, unless the distribution is to the surviving spouse. You can distribute personal items and modest cash bequests provided you retain enough for an equalization claim, dependant's support, and other potential claims. If a claim is filed, you should seek legal advice on how to proceed. Although the right to claim equalization is relatively straightforward, the calculation and valuations of property can be complicated.

Dependant support claims

In addition to an equalization claim, a surviving spouse, and any other person who meets the definition of a "dependant," can make a claim for dependant support against the estate. Under the *Succession Law Reform Act* the estate can be ordered to make adequate provision for a dependant. "Dependant" means a spouse, parent, child, or sibling of the deceased, to whom the deceased either was providing support or was under a legal obligation to provide support immediately before death. "Spouse" includes couples who have cohabited continuously for three years or more and couples in a relationship of some permanence who are the natural or adoptive parents of a child. [9]

---

[9] *Succession Law Reform Act*, R.S.O. 1990, c. S.26, Part V.

The amount of support is based on numerous factors in section 62 of the *Succession Law Reform Act*—essentially, a balance of the needs of the dependant and the ability of the estate to pay. The factors also include compensatory support, by subsections "(h) the contributions made by the dependant to the deceased's welfare, including indirect and non-financial contributions; (i) the contributions made by the dependant to the acquisition, maintenance and improvement of the deceased's property or business; (j) a contribution by the dependant to the realization of the deceased's career potential; and (r) (iii) the effect on the spouse's earning capacity of the responsibilities assumed during cohabitation."

The court can order a lump sum or ongoing payments, or that specific property be transferred to the dependant, either outright, in trust, for life, for a period, or as security for the payment of support.

No application for support can be made after six months from the grant of a Certificate of Appointment of Estate Trustee (i.e. probate). However, this can be extended under subsection 61(2) of the Act as to any portion of the estate remaining undistributed as at the date of the application.

Constructive and Resulting Trusts

A spouse or partner, or any person for that matter, can assert a claim for a "constructive trust" against the deceased's estate. Or, the estate can assert a constructive trust against another person. A constructive trust can arise where one person contributes value to another person's property without compensation. Such contributions can arise among married spouses, common law spouses, or in other relationships. The classic cases in the family law context are when one spouse has title to a farm or a business and the other spouse contributes for many years without compensation. To remedy the "unjust enrichment" on marriage breakup or death, the court can declare that the legal owner holds some or all of the beneficial interest of the property in trust for the contributor. These remedies are in addition to any family law equalization claim, but if awarded, would be taken into account when equalizing properties. These claims can also arise in a business context where one person contributes to another person's property without compensation and that person is "unjustly enriched" without "juristic reason."

In addition to a constructive trust, the estate may face a resulting trust. A "resulting trust" can exist when one person transfers property to, or buys property in the name of, another without economic value in return. The presumption is that a gift was not intended and beneficial ownership remains with the transferor. (The exception is that a transfer into the joint names of married spouses is presumed to be beneficially owned jointly by the couple.) The classic example in an estate context is where an elderly person adds one of her adult children on title as a joint owner to her bank account, so that her child can do her banking, pay her bills, and assist with her finances. When the elderly person dies, title to the bank account would be recorded in the name of the adult child as the survivor, but the adult child is presumed to hold the funds in trust for the elderly person's estate. Similarly, where an elderly person puts her child on title to her investments to avoid probate tax or adds her child as a joint owner to her house, the presumption at law is that the adult child holds that property in trust for the estate. The adult child would have the legal burden to prove that the intention of the elderly person was not that it would revert to the estate, but that the surviving adult child would in fact own the entire property on her death. At the time of writing, there is a recent Ontario case which has held that the designated recipient of an RRSP or RRIF holds those funds for the estate on a resulting trust, unless there is an expressed intention otherwise.[10]

These legal principles are well-known among estate lawyers, and if you believe that a trust may arise in the context of the estate that you are administering, then seek professional advice.

Marriage or cohabitation agreements

Pre- and post-marriage contracts and cohabitation agreements can define property and support rights, can secure a survivor's right to occupy a home or receive a specified income, and can secure capital for the children if income is to be used for a surviving spouse. However, a provision in a marriage contract purporting to limit a spouse's rights under Part II of the *Family Law Act* regarding the matrimonial home is unenforceable.[11] Similarly, two persons who are cohabiting or intend to cohabit and who are not married to each other may enter into an agreement in which they agree on their respective

---

[10] *Calmusky v. Calmusky*, 2020 ONSC 1506

[11] *Family Law Act, supra* note 5 s 55(2).

rights and obligations during cohabitation, or on ceasing to cohabit or on death.

Before distributing any funds from the estate, you should review any marriage or cohabitation agreement that could apply. It may be that the distribution plan in the will is inconsistent with the agreement. For instance, the agreement could have required the deceased to have maintained life insurance to fund support, and if that did not happen, the spouse can claim damages against the estate.

Mutual wills claim

You should be cautious when administering an estate in which the will-maker had a mirror will with their spouse. Mirror wills contain terms that are mirror images of each other with the same distribution plan drafted by the same lawyer. Usually, the spouses leave everything to the survivor, and when they both die, the remainder is to be distributed equally among their children. Sometimes, after the first spouse dies, the survivor will draft a new will with a new distribution plan. A will is normally a revocable instrument and the survivor can do this unless there is a binding agreement that says otherwise. The agreement must amount to a contract in law, it must be proven by clear evidence, and it must include an agreement not to revoke their wills without notifying or obtaining the consent of the other. A mutual wills agreement need not be written but can be implied from the circumstances supported or negated by extrinsic evidence. The onus is on the party alleging the doctrine of mutual wills to prove the existence of the agreement.

When there is such an agreement, the mirror wills are mutual wills, the survivor can deal with the inherited property without restriction if doing so is not inconsistent with the intent of the agreement. If the survivor, after taking a benefit, alters their will or disposes of property in a way that violates the terms of the agreement, the estate trustee must hold the property upon a constructive trust to perform the contract and the original will. The issue is complex, and if it arises in the estate that you are administering, you should seek professional advice.

Business contracts

The deceased may have been a shareholder in a private corporation, or a partner in a business partnership, which requires that the estate sell the deceased's shares or interest in accordance with a valuation procedure. To fund such a purchase, often the corporation or partnership will carry life insurance on the deceased. The terms of such agreements should be carefully reviewed.

Personal injury claim

If the deceased died because of the negligence of another, such as a careless driver or a negligent medical professional, you should retain a personal injury lawyer to pursue the claim. Others may join the claim, such as family who have lost financial support or suffered emotional or other damages. This should be carefully considered.

Continuation of a claim

If the deceased had filed a claim, or a claim had been made against the deceased, then it continues after death and you are to file a court document confirming your authority to act on behalf of the estate. To do so and to obtain a judgment from the court, you must first obtain a Certificate of Appointment of Estate Trustee (probate).

Limitation periods

If you think that litigation is a possibility, you should note the limitation periods. The general limitation period in Ontario is two years from the date that the plaintiff first knew of the injury or loss, or two years from the date that a reasonable person ought to have known of the claim, whichever is earlier.[12] In addition, no court action can be taken for an unpaid account, debt, contract, or civil wrong against the estate, after two years of the date of death.[13]

Court process

The litigation process is complicated and time-consuming, and a lawyer should carefully guide you through it. The main steps in the litigation process are: a claim or application is prepared and filed; the claim or application is served; the party served prepares and files a response; discoveries take place, which can include "Examinations for Discovery," where each party is questioned by the opposing lawyer(s), on the record, in the presence of a Court Reporter; mandatory mediation takes place; the action or application is set down for trial; a pre-trial conference is held, and then a trial takes place. Most civil cases do not make it to trial. The mediation hearing can be an excellent way to resolve matters without incurring excessive costs.

---

[12] *Limitations Act*, 2002, S.O. 2002, c. 24, Sched. B, s 5.
[13] *Trustee Act*, R.S.O. 1990, c. T.23, s 38(3).

Chapter Eight—Income tax returns

This chapter is *not* intended to be a detailed explanation of income tax planning. Rather, it highlights some of the income tax returns that need to be filed. It was written with the assistance of Brian Quinlan and Dickson Lai, chartered professional accountants at the Toronto firm of Campbell Lawless LLP (camlaw.on.ca), and they are available for a free initial consultation. An accountant should be retained to file the income tax returns for the deceased and for the estate. As the estate trustee, you are personally responsible for the payment of any income taxes up to the amount that funds are available in the estate. The cost to retain an accountant to file the tax returns represents a legitimate expense to be paid by the estate.

Personal income tax returns

The personal income tax returns (tax form T1) to be filed for the deceased are:

- any unfiled personal income tax returns for the years before the year of death, and
- a personal income tax return for the year of death which is referred to as the final (or terminal) personal income tax return.

Additional and optional separate personal income tax returns which can be filed in the year of death are:

- a personal income tax return for *rights and things*,
- a personal income tax return when the deceased was a beneficiary of an estate that was a *graduated rate estate*, and

- a personal income tax return when the deceased had been self-employed and earned income through a partnership or proprietorship with a non-calendar year end.

By filing separate tax returns in the year of death, the use of graduated tax brackets can be maximized. Also, by filing separate tax returns, certain income tax credits can be claimed more than once.

Final personal income tax return of the deceased

The final personal income tax return reports the income earned from January 1st of the year of death up to the date of death. The tax return and tax payments are due on April 30th of the following year where the deceased died on or before October 31st. Where the death occurred after October 31st, the tax return and payments are due six months after the death. If the deceased was self-employed, and if the death was on or before December 15th, the final personal income tax return is not due until June 15th of the following year.

Deemed disposition of assets on death, other than RRSPs, RRIFs and TFSAs

At death, a taxpayer is deemed to have sold all of their unregistered assets (i.e. not RRSPs and not RRIFs) at a price equal to the fair market value at the time, i.e. the deceased has a "deemed sale" or "deemed disposition" of all of their assets. Fifty percent of the resulting net capital gains (capital gains in excess of *permitted* capital losses) are taxable in the final personal income tax return of the deceased.

Generally, capital losses may be claimed only to reduce capital gains that are subject to income tax. Where a taxpayer – deceased or not – incurs a permitted capital loss in a year, and there are no capital gains (realized or deemed to be realized) in the same year, the loss can be applied to offset capital gains reported as far back as three years. A special income tax provision permits the deceased, in computing taxable income in the year of death, to deduct the unused net capital losses (which are fifty percent of the actual capital losses) against any other types of income—employment, self-employment, pension and/or investment income—including any income inclusion resulting from RRSPs and RRIFs being deregistered on death.

The amount of capital losses that can be deducted in the year of death is reduced where the taxpayer has made use of the capital gains exemption. Many taxpayers made use of the exemption by filing a capital gain election with their 1994 personal income tax return as part of the $100,000 capital gains exemption phase out. Canada Revenue Agency can provide the history on a taxpayer's past use of the capital gains exemption.

Principal residence exemption

The principal residence exemption can be used to shelter all or a portion of the accrued capital gain on the deceased's residence. Until 1981, it was possible for both spouses to claim the principal residence exemption on separate family properties. Since 1981, only one family property is eligible. If the deceased owned more than one residence, such as a city house and a cottage, the principal residence exemption should generally be used for the property with the highest accrued capital gain.

In determining the tax cost of a family-use property that has been held for a long time, the beginning point is the value of the property on January 1, 1972. (There was no income tax on capital gains before 1972.) The tax cost is then increased by capital improvements made to the property. Also, many individuals made use of the 1994 capital gains election to increase the tax cost of a family-use property. (This was usually done in respect of the family's cottage property, as it was expected that the principal residence exemption would be used in respect of the sale, or deemed sale on death, of the family's city home.)

Personal-use property

Also subject to income tax on death are capital gains from the deemed dispositions of personal-use property—e.g. cars and boats. If there are accrued losses, then the capital losses cannot be used. Also, capital loss on one personal-use asset cannot be used to offset a capital gain on another personal-use asset. However, capital losses on personal-use property that qualifies as "listed personal property"— e.g., art, jewelry, rare books, stamps and coins—are permitted to be claimed against other listed personal property assets, but only to the extent that they offset any capital gains incurred on other listed personal property.

The minimum value to use in calculating the gains and losses on personal-use property for both the deemed market value at time of death and the tax cost is $1,000.

RRSP and RRIF accounts held at death

When the deceased had an RRSP or RRIF account, these plans are considered to be *de-registered* on death resulting in all of the value being taxable on the deceased's final personal income tax return.

TFSA account held at death

Assets held in a TFSA at death remain tax-free to the deceased.

Transfer of assets to a surviving spouse

When assets (those *not* held in an RRSP or RRIF) are passed on death to the deceased's spouse (which includes a common-law spouse), no income tax will arise on the death of the first spouse. This is because there is a default income tax rule that provides that the deceased has not had a "deemed sale" or "deemed disposition" of assets at market value. Rather, the assets are "rolled over" to the surviving spouse at their tax cost and no capital gain will arise on the death of the first spouse.

Sometimes, it is better if the default income tax rule does *not* apply; for example, if the deceased has realized capital losses in the year of death or has unused capital losses being carried forward from previous years. These losses cannot be passed to a surviving spouse, or to any other beneficiary for that matter. Here it is best to "elect out" of the default income tax rule to permit an accrued capital gain to be realized which can then be sheltered by the capital losses of the deceased. Other cases where it may be preferred to elect out of the default rule include where the deceased at the time of death owned shares of a small business or owned a farm or a fishing property that qualifies for the capital gains exemption. There are also other situations where it is best to intentionally trigger some or all of the capital gains on death. These options should be reviewed with your tax professional.

Transfer of an RRSP or RRIF account to a surviving spouse

The deceased will *not* be subject to tax on the value of an RRSP or RRIF at death to the extent the RRSP or RRIF account is:

- transferred to a surviving spouse;
- transferred to a financially dependent child or grandchild; or
- transferred to a Registered Disability Savings Plan (RDSP) of a financially dependent child or grandchild.

When the beneficiary of an RRSP or RRIF is a financially dependent child or grandchild of the deceased, the value of the RRSP or RRIF is taxed in the hands of the dependant rather than the deceased. If the child or grandchild is under eighteen, the tax can be spread over the number of years remaining until the child is eighteen with the purchase of an annuity.

If the financial dependency is due to a physical or mental disability, the dependant can avoid being immediately taxed on the RRSP or RRIF proceeds by making a transfer to their own RRSP or RRIF or using the funds to purchase an annuity. Income tax is then paid only by the dependant as withdrawals are made from the RRSP or RRIF or when an annuity payment is received.

A deceased taxpayer can also defer income tax on the value of an RRSP or RRIF at death where the proceeds are transferred to a RDSP (registered disability savings plan) of a financially dependent child or grandchild. The amount transferred to the RDSP cannot cause the beneficiary's maximum RDSP contribution room of $200,000 to be exceeded and no Canada Disability Savings Grant is paid on the transfer. The beneficiary of the RDSP will pay income tax as amounts are withdrawn from the RDSP.

Income tax return for the estate of the deceased

In addition to the personal income tax returns, you must file an estate tax return for income earned after the date of death, called a "trust income tax and information return" (tax form T3). The number of yearly estate income tax returns to be filed will depend on how quickly the estate is wound-up and when the assets are distributed to the estate's beneficiaries.

The estate can be designated as a graduated rate estate ("GRE") for thirty-six months following the deceased's death. If designated, the estate can make use of the graduated income tax rates and can choose an off-calendar taxation year-end. In addition, any charitable donation tax credits can be used in the year the donation is made or in the following five years, in a previous tax year of the GRE, in the deceased's final tax return, or in the deceased's tax return for the year prior to death. There are other tax advantages for a GRE which should be reviewed with your tax professional. Only one GRE can exist for the deceased's estate.

Tax clearance certificate

Before making a final distribution from the estate, you should obtain a "tax clearance certificate" from the Canada Revenue Agency, to confirm that all income taxes (personal and estate) have been paid. If you fail to do so, you may be personally liable for these income taxes.

Chapter Nine—Estate Transfers

Review the terms of the will

Some wills allow you to distribute personal property or other assets directly to the beneficiaries, rather than to sell assets and distribute only cash. This is an example in a will precedent:

> "Instead of selling assets to realize money and then distributing only money to the beneficiaries, you may distribute estate assets to the beneficiaries as part or all of their shares in the estate; you may determine the market value of those assets and the value shall be binding on the beneficiaries."

Although this clause would allow you to determine market values, beneficiaries would have a valid complaint if you did not act reasonably. Therefore, you should obtain independent valuations of the more significant assets prior to distributing.

Personal items

Some wills allow flexibility when distributing personal items among the family, as discussed in chapter five. One strategy is to circulate a list of items and confidentially ask family members what items they would like to receive and in which priority. Another strategy is to give family members a pecking order (perhaps in order of age) to take turns choosing personal items. Personal items can trigger emotional attachments, and so, to the extent possible, it is important to achieve harmony or at least a sense of fairness.

If personal items of value remain undistributed, then consider an estate auction, either online or through an estate auction house. Get expert advice for valuable items.

Vehicles and Boats

You may be required to transfer vehicles or boats to beneficiaries. To transfer a vehicle, you must bring a notarized copy of the will, death certificate, and ownership information to Service Ontario. If no will exists, a letter from a lawyer confirming who is the beneficiary of the vehicle should be enough. You should contact Service Ontario to determine their requirements.

Real estate

Real estate can be registered in different ways, the most common of which are "joint tenants" and "tenants in common". If the deceased was a joint tenant, the survivor can register 100% ownership with a death certificate. If the deceased was a tenant in common, then probate will probably be required to transfer the deceased's interest. See chapter five.

If the deceased held title jointly with someone who survived, determine if the surviving owner is holding ownership of some or all of the property on a resulting trust for the estate, as described in chapter seven.

Unless it was the deceased's principal residence, obtain evidence of the purchase price of the real estate, the cost of any capital improvements, the value when the deceased died, and the current value if the deceased died some years ago. You need this information to calculate the capital gains tax, even if there is a joint tenant with survivorship rights. If so, the deceased's capital gain would be calculated based on the deceased's ownership interest as of the day before death. See chapter eight. You should send this information to your accountant so that the income tax returns may be completed.

Consider whether one or more of the properties were a matrimonial home. As discussed in chapters five and seven, the surviving spouse may have equalization rights to one-half of the value of the home (or homes), regardless of when the home was purchased during the marriage, and the surviving spouse may also have possessory rights. A spouse who has no interest in a matrimonial home but is occupying it at the time of the other spouse's death, whether under an order for exclusive possession or otherwise, is entitled to retain possession against the spouse's estate, rent free, for sixty days after the spouse's death.[1]

Sometimes, the will gives a surviving spouse or adult children an option to purchase the real estate from the estate. This is common for family cottages, where the emotional attachment to a property can exceed its market value. The following is an example clause:

> "If my daughter Jenna survives me, she shall have the option to include the cottage in her share of the remainder of my estate at the market value of the cottage. To exercise the option, within six months of my death, Jenna must give written notice to my Estate Trustee to do so ("Jenna's notice"). For this purpose, the market value of the cottage shall be as agreed by Jenna and my Estate Trustee. If they do

---

[1] *Family Law Act*, R.S.O. 1990, c. F.3 s26(2).

not agree on the market value of the cottage within two months of Jenna's notice, the market value shall be the average of two appraisals, with each of Jenna and my Estate Trustee selecting a qualified, independent, professional appraiser to provide an appraisal of the market value of the cottage."

Sometimes the will gives the surviving spouse or adult child who was living in the house a period to remain living there, rent-free, or sometimes with a contribution to utilities or property taxes, before listing the property for sale. This is to allow the survivor(s) a transition time.

If there are no restrictions on selling the property, you should retain a real estate agent to sell the property. You could sell the property privately without an agent to save on the real estate commission, but the risk is that you may sell the property below the market price and the beneficiaries could later complain. (If the property is to be sold privately, consider obtaining the written consent of all the beneficiaries to the terms of the sale before doing so.)

The real estate agent will require that you sign a listing agreement, in which the agent is normally given exclusive rights to sell the property for a period of time. Have this agreement reviewed by a real estate lawyer, to determine whether the period of exclusive listing is reasonable and whether the commission charged is market rate. This is important, since the agent may have "earned" their commission if they obtain an offer at the listing price during the term, even if you later decide that the price is too low.

The process of selling is normally left to the real estate lawyer, who will review the title and arrange to pay off any outstanding mortgages or liens. The net proceeds could be paid into the estate account, but if that is done, then probate will likely be required to release those funds later. Alternatively, the funds could be held in the solicitor's trust account, if arrangements could be made with the solicitor to release funds on your direction. Probate will likely be required to sell the property if title was registered solely in the deceased's name. See chapter five.

The Family Business

If the deceased owned a business, then review all shareholder, employment, consulting, banking, debt, and other business agreements.

If the business is a corporation with multiple shareholders, determine whether there is a shareholders' agreement. A shareholders' agreement will normally include buy-sell provisions that are triggered on death. Often, the business or other shareholders will carry life insurance to fund the payout. If the price of the shares is not set out in the agreement, an issue becomes what price are the deceased's shares worth? The concept of "market value" is simple enough, but in a small business, in which the shares do not trade on the market, and in which the value of the business may diminish because the founder has died, it can be a contentious issue. Business valuators can agree about methodologies but arrive at different payout amounts.

If someone else in the family was involved in the business, the will may give them an option to purchase the shares from the estate. Again, what are those shares worth?

If no one has the option or obligation to purchase the deceased's shares, then you should determine how to sell ("liquidate") those shares as soon as possible for the highest profit. It may be best to continue the business for a period, managed by a trusted employee or outside professional, before selling the business. A "fire sale" may not yield the best price. Running the business for a period can establish that it has a value apart from its now deceased owner, so that a buyer will feel more confident that it can continue to generate profits. There is a risk, however, that running an unprofitable business will increase its liabilities and make the shares less valuable.

If the deceased's business was an active Canadian small business corporation, there are tax issues to consider. It may qualify for the $883,384 (as at 2020) capital gains exemption. A farm or fishing property may qualify for the $1,000,000 capital gains exemption. These exemptions should be used, rather than transferred to the surviving spouse. The surviving spouse will have a higher tax cost for the property received, reducing the subsequent capital gains tax for the surviving spouse. Review these issues with the accountant.

Registered Investments

The deceased may have had Registered Retirement Savings Plans (RRSPs) or Registered Retirement Income Funds (RRIFs). These are tax-deferred plans in which income tax is payable only on withdrawal of funds. On death, these plans are considered to be *de-registered* resulting in all of their value being taxable. There are tax-free transfers to a surviving spouse, and certain savings to a dependent child. See chapter eight.

Usually the registered plan will designate who is to receive on the holder's death. If so, then the proceeds of the registered plan go directly to the beneficiary, and not through the estate. This will normally save probate tax (the tax is applied only to the value of assets flowing through the will probated with the court). If the designation is not to a surviving spouse, then there can be significant income taxes to pay, and those taxes are payable in the deceased's final personal income tax return, reducing the value of the estate. The beneficiary receives the proceeds tax-free, unless there are insufficient assets in the estate to pay the personal income tax of the deceased.

Sometimes the beneficiary of a registered plan has agreed in advance to hold funds received in trust, either for the estate or for beneficiaries. This should be reviewed.

To trigger the payment, send the financial institution a notarized copy of the death certificate, with directions as to the location of the beneficiary. Additional documents may need to be delivered.

Tax Free Savings Accounts (TFSAs)

The deceased may have had a Tax Free Savings Account (TFSA). Assets held in a TFSA at death remain tax-free to the deceased. If a TFSA holder names their spouse or common-law partner as the successor holder, then on the death of the TFSA holder, the spouse becomes the new holder and the tax-exempt status of the TFSA is maintained. All of this is done without affecting the TFSA contribution room of the surviving spouse. The rules are somewhat different if the spouse is named the beneficiary of the TFSA.

Life insurance

Like registered plans, life insurance documents will usually designate who is to receive on the insured's death. If so, then the proceeds of the life insurance go directly to the beneficiary, and not through the estate. This will save probate tax.

Sometimes the beneficiary of a life insurance plan has agreed in advance to hold funds received in trust, either for the estate or for beneficiaries. This should be reviewed.

To trigger the payment, send the life insurance company a notarized copy of the death certificate, with directions as to the location of the beneficiary. The life insurance company may require additional documentation.

Pension Plans

The deceased may have had a pension plan which pays a survivor's or dependant's pension after the employee's death. If so, those payouts go directly to the surviving spouse or dependant and are not included in the estate assets. They are included in the surviving spouse's or dependant's personal income tax returns when received.

Where there is no survivor, some pension plans include a payout of pension credits to a designated beneficiary. Similarly, those payouts do not go through the estate and are not included in the estate assets.

The payout is included in the recipient's personal income tax return when received.

Although these payments do not go through the estate, you should take steps to assist the beneficiary to receive these payments.

Intellectual property and "Digital Assets"

There has been much discussion about digital assets and how they should be transferred in an estate. It is common for a deceased to have subscribed to multiple online memberships or services, with monthly fees, which you should cancel.

The simplest solution is for the deceased to have recorded all of their passwords in a safe place, and share access to these passwords with you, or at least, leave instructions with their will as to how to gain access to these passwords. If the deceased failed to do this and you have no access to the passwords, you must send the various accounts a copy of the death certificate and a letter requiring that the account be closed.

Other intellectual property that was owned by the deceased can be copyright, trademarks, or patents, registered in Canada or elsewhere. You should search the deceased's and the public records to see if and when renewals are required to preserve property rights. Later, you can sell those assets, if valuable.

Chapter Ten—Distributions and Releases

By now, you should have collected all or most of the estate assets (chapters two and five), determined the liabilities (chapter six), determined any possible claims for or against the estate (chapter seven), calculated the income tax (chapter eight), and the estate administration tax (chapter four). If you have done all of this, you may be able to do a partial or interim distribution.

Partial or interim distribution

Do not distribute all of the estate assets until you are certain that all of the liabilities and taxes have been paid and that the limitation period for any potential lawsuit has expired. You should leave money in the estate because you can be personally liable for any shortfall.

If the deceased was married, you should *not* do an interim distribution within the first six months after death, unless it is a partial distribution to the surviving married spouse. The surviving married spouse has six months to file an equalization claim (unless a court agrees to extend the limitation period). You should also delay a distribution until six months after probate is issued if there is any possibility of a claim by a dependant, such as a spouse, common-law partner, dependant child, or dependant sibling. See chapter seven. If probate is not required, you should leave some funds in reserve for a longer period for a possible dependant support claim.

No court action can be taken for an unpaid account, debt, contract, or civil wrong against the estate, two years after the date of death.[1] (See chapter six) This is a "limitation period." In addition, there is a two year limitation period from when the cause of action arose, which would likely expire sooner. You should leave funds in reserve for any possible claim.

You are responsible for filing the income tax returns and for any deficiency for past year filings (see chapter eight). After filing the returns, the Canada Revenue Agency ("CRA") will issue a Notice of Assessment. However, the CRA will change the assessment if it later determines that there was an error. If this happens, the CRA will issue a Notice of Reassessment.

You can obtain and rely on a tax clearance certificate from the CRA, as, once it is issued, the CRA is prevented from re-assessing any income tax return, unless the information provided to the CRA was false or incomplete. This is why, if you do an interim distribution, it should be a partial distribution and you should reserve more than enough funds until you receive a tax clearance certificate. The tax clearance certificate is for a specific tax filing, rather than a general release. Thus, you should obtain a tax clearance certificate that includes the final personal tax return of the deceased and any income tax returns filed by the estate.

---

[1] *Trustee Act*, R.S.O. 1990, c. T.23, s 38(3).

You are also responsible for the Estate Administration Tax return and for any deficiency. Unlike income tax and the CRA, there is no tax clearance certificate available to protect you from liability. That said, the calculation and assessment of the Estate Administration Tax is much simpler than income tax.

Legacies

A legacy is a cash or specific amount of gift to a beneficiary. The following is an example of a legacy: "Give $5,000 to my sister Rosa if she survives me." A legacy can also be an amount that is contingent on the sale of an asset: "Sell my boat and give the net proceeds to my son Jamar if he survives me."

Usually, the will prioritizes the payment of legacies, and the residue or remainder of the estate (discussed below) is distributed to the these beneficiaries only after all the debts, taxes, administration expenses, and legacies have been paid. If there are insufficient assets in the estate, then the legacies may have to be decreased. Which legacies should be decreased, and by how much, will depend on the deceased's intention as expressed in the wording of the will. If all the legacies are grouped in order, such that they appear to be of equal importance, the legacies will be decreased proportionately. If, however, the will prioritizes certain legacies over other legacies, they are to be paid in priority.

If it becomes clear that the estate has enough assets to pay all the legacies, they should be paid within a reasonable time. What is reasonable varies, but you should normally pay the legacies within the "Executor's year," which is an expression that means you have one year from the date of death to collect all assets, pay all liabilities, and distribute the assets to the beneficiaries. For this reason, a beneficiary of a cash bequest (e.g. "Give $5,000 to my sister Rosa if she survives me") can demand interest on the legacy after one year of the death. In normal circumstances, there is no reason to delay payment of legacies. The residuary beneficiaries may have to wait for their full payment, but not the legacies.

When the asset is gone—ademption

If the will makes a gift of a specific asset that cannot be found after death, the gift fails or "adeems." This applies if the asset was lost, destroyed, sold, given away, or changed into another form.

However, the rule has been modified somewhat by section 20 of the *Succession Law Reform Act*, by tracing the gift to the proceeds or security received by the will-maker. Also, if the asset was given away by an attorney under a continuing power of attorney, then the would-be beneficiary is entitled to receive from the residue of the estate the equivalent of a corresponding right in the proceeds of the disposition of the property, without interest.[2]

If the beneficiary dies first—lapse

Be careful when gifts are made to beneficiaries who died before the will-maker, because different rules apply depending on the circumstances. If a gift is made to someone who dies before the will-maker, unless a contrary intention appears in the will, the gift usually fails or "lapses" and would normally be distributed in accordance with the residuary clause in the will, if there is one.[3] This is not true

---

[2] *Substitute Decisions Act*, 1992, S.O. 1992, c. 30, s 36(1).

for bequests made to a child, grandchild, or sibling of the will-maker; unless a contrary intention appears in the will, those gifts take effect as though they had been made directly to the intended beneficiary's survivors.[4]

If the beneficiary had already received their gift before the deceased died

You should review the deceased's notes and records to see whether they had made significant gifts or loans to a beneficiary, because these might reduce the amounts to which that beneficiary is entitled. There is legal presumption against double portions called "ademption by advancement." If, after signing their will and before they died, the deceased made a gift that is substantial or equivalent in nature to the gift or legacy provided for in the will, typically to one of their children (this rule does not apply to a gift to a spouse), the law presumes that this gift was an advance on the gift from the estate. If so, then the child's share of the estate will be reduced by the amount of the advancement. However, there will be no ademption or reduction if the evidence shows that the deceased intended that the child would receive both benefits. A way to show this intention is through a specific provision in the will, such as the following: "None of my beneficiaries shall be liable to bring into account any money, or the value of property, that I may have transferred to any of them prior to my death unless I have indicated in writing at the time of the transfer that is not to be a gift."

---

[3] *Succession Law Reform Act*, R.S.O. 1990, c. S.26, s 23.
[4] *Ibid*, s. 31.

What is the "residue"?

An estate can have several remainders or residues. There is the remainder of the whole estate—what is left after all the other provisions in the will are satisfied. There is also the remainder of an ongoing testamentary trust. Sometimes the remainder of a particular trust is added to the general remainder. This should all be set out in the will.

Per stirpes / Per capita—what is the difference?

Often, the will leaves everything to the surviving spouse, and if the spouse has already died, equally among their children. If one of the children has died, usually the will says that the gift that the deceased child would have received is to be shared equally among those grandchildren. There are two common ways to share among the next generation, *per capita* and *per stirpes*:

Per capita— "By the head"—each grandchild receives the same amount from the estate.

Per stirpes— "By the branch" or "By representation"—the share that each child would have received is divided equally among the next generation of that branch.

For example: The deceased had three children: Curly, Larry, and Moe. All three died before the deceased. Curly had no children, Larry had one child (Laura, who is alive), and Moe had two children (Matthew and Mark, who are both alive).

Per capita—Laura, Matthew and Mark each receive one-third.

Per stirpes—Laura receives 50%, Matthew receives 25%, and Mark receives 25%.

Loss of right to inherit

The Ontario court has the power to disentitle a beneficiary if the gift offends public policy. This was discussed in chapter seven under "Gifts which are void as against public policy." In addition, even though the wording of the will may not be offensive, the gift can become void if the beneficiary committed some act that offends public policy, such as murdering the deceased to receive their inheritance early.

Priorities when distributing the remainder

The intention expressed in the will determines what priorities, if any, apply to the distribution of an estate. You are not to favour one beneficiary over another, unless the will requires it. Normally, the remainder interests are given a percentage or share, and so the calculation is determined accordingly.

Obtain releases from beneficiaries

A beneficiary who is to receive a specific cash legacy need only provide a receipt when paid. If payment is made more than one year after the death, then you should obtain a release from any claim for interest.

If the beneficiary is under the age of eighteen years, then review the will to determine who can accept payment on behalf of the child. A child cannot legally provide a release. Some wills allow for payment to the child's parent. A guardian of property for the child can receive payment, but the child's parent is not automatically the guardian. If no such method is described, and if the payment is significant, you may need to make payment into court for the account of the child.

A beneficiary who is to receive a share or percentage of the estate, or a share or percentage of part of the estate, is entitled to a full accounting of all assets, liabilities, taxes and costs, so that the beneficiary can be satisfied that their share was properly administered. Details on estate accounting are provided in chapter thirteen.

All beneficiaries who are entitled to a share or a percentage of the estate should sign a release similar to the following. If any beneficiary has a mental capacity issue, their guardian or attorney for property should sign on their behalf, and if there is no such person, then the Public Guardian and Trustee should review on their behalf.

Form of Interim Release:

The following is a draft form of interim release. It requires that the beneficiary also receives a complete summary of the accounts for all matters to the date of the release, and an opportunity to access all supporting documents and invoices. If you fail to provide full disclosure, the release becomes virtually meaningless.

On receipt of $***** the undersigned, John Fiction.

Approves the accounting and first interim distribution proposal of the Estate Trustee set out in a Summary dated August 30, 2020, for the period since Jack Fiction died on June 1, 2020 to the date of September 30, 2020;

Releases and discharges the Estate Trustee, her agents, associates and representatives, successors and assigns of and from any and all actions, causes of actions, claims, demands for damages or loss, however arising, including all claims for costs including all damage or loss which may arise in the future, arising from all matters having to do with the administration of the Estate for the period from June 1, 2020 to the date of September 30, 2020.

I confirm that I have been provided full disclosure of the accounts of the Estate to the date of September 30, 2020, with access to all supporting documents to support the summary.

I confirm that I have been advised to retain independent legal advice before signing this release.

Non resident beneficiaries

If the beneficiary is not a Canadian resident, then determine what tax documentation is required. Although there is no gift tax to the recipient in Canada, there may be a gift tax to the recipient in other countries. You should discuss these issues with a tax advisor.

Chapter 11—Estates with no Will

Many people die without a will. There is a myth that the government will seize the deceased's property if there is no will. Instead, there is a default "intestate" distribution method among the closest relatives. If no one acceptable steps forward to act as the estate trustee, the government Public Guardian and Trustee will administer the estate for the family and dependants.

Who inherits if there is no will?

If the deceased has no will, the estate is to be distributed according to the rules of intestacy contained in Part II of Ontario's *Succession Law Reform Act.* The Act prescribes the following: If there is a married spouse but no children, the spouse will receive everything. If there is both a married spouse and children, the spouse will receive the first $200,000 (under the current regulation) and the balance will be divided among the spouse and the children according to a formula (one-half to the spouse if there is one child, and one-third to the spouse and two-thirds to the children if there is more than one child). If there are children and no surviving spouse, then all goes to the children. If there is no spouse and no children, then all goes to the parents, whom failing to the siblings, whom failing to the grandparents, whom failing to the cousins, etc., "among the next of kin of equal degree of consanguinity."

As estate trustee, you have a duty to locate the closest relatives. This may be easy if the spouse and the children are all living under the same roof, but the definition of "children" includes blood children from any relationship (see below), and wayward children may be difficult to locate. You should search Ontario's Registrar General for parentage. It can become difficult if the closest relatives are the cousins of the deceased, some of whom may live overseas. If there is uncertainty whether all of the closest relatives have been located, you should apply to court for approval of the list of relatives, with evidence of the reasonable steps you have taken to locate all who may be entitled to receive.

Who administers the estate if there is no will?

The court will appoint an "Estate Trustee Without a Will." Normally, the court will appoint someone whom the survivors agree is best able to administer the estate. If the survivors cannot agree, the court will likely appoint the spouse, whom failing the adult children, whom failing a parent or sibling of the deceased. If no one acceptable steps forward, the Public Guardian and Trustee is appointed. The estate trustee must be a resident of Ontario.

If either the spouse or a dependant intends to commence litigation against the estate for net family property equalization or dependant support, the spouse or dependant is in a conflict of interest and should not be appointed the estate trustee.

In most cases, the estate trustee will be required to post an administration bond with the court at twice the estimated value of the estate. This is to protect the beneficiaries if the estate trustee is either negligent or fraudulent. The cost of the bond will be paid by the estate. An application can be made to dispense with the bond, which is usually granted if the court is shown that the estate trustee has a good financial record, that there are more than enough assets for any creditors and dependents of the estate, the beneficiaries are all adults, mentally capable, and have all consented to the appointment in writing.

Litigation when there is no will

The lack of a will does not prevent litigation; in fact, it can make litigation more likely, especially if the spouse is unsatisfied with their share through intestacy. The surviving spouse can file a net family property equalization claim against the estate, just as though there were a will. Similarly, the spouse or other dependant can file a claim for support. Claims for both "constructive" and "resulting" trusts can be made. The same litigation principles apply as though there were a will. See chapter seven.

Adopted children / stepchildren / half-blood relatives

The rules of intestacy are inclusive. Blood relatives, including children born outside of marriage, and legally adopted children inherit on an intestacy. Legally adopted children are included and treated the same as biological children. Half-blood relatives share equally with whole-blood relatives.[1]

If the deceased is a man who had an affair years before his death, without realizing that he had become a father, then that person would be the deceased's child for the purposes of intestacy. In addition, for the purposes of intestacy and dependant support, the definition of a child in the *Succession Law Reform Act* includes a child born after the father's death.

---

[1] Half-blood relatives are those that only share one common ancestor with the deceased while whole blood relatives share two.

Under Ontario's *All Families are Equal Act*, a person who donates sperm or an embryo through artificial means is not a parent, unless the person was married to the birth parent or other conditions apply.

Chapter 12—Transfers to ongoing trusts

There are two phases of the administration of an estate. In the first phase, you are to assemble the deceased's assets, pay the debts and administration costs, and distribute what is left to the beneficiaries. You have a reasonable time to do so (sometimes called the "Executor's year").

If the estate has ongoing trusts to administer, then there is a second phase, which can last for many years. There may be a trust for the spouse or common-law partner for life, a child until a stated age, or even a parent. The trustee of an ongoing trust can be the estate trustee, or someone else. What follows is a description of some of the more common "testamentary" trusts that arise out of a will.

Note: Until 2016, there was a tax benefit in multiplying the number of testamentary trusts. This was because the income earned in each testamentary trust was subject to the graduated rates of tax. Thus, income taxes could be saved if a parent or adult child had a testamentary trust, which, along with their personal income tax returns, would multiply the number of graduated rate tax returns resulting in a lower overall rate of tax, year over year. However, in 2016, the tax rules changed and now, only one trust in the estate enjoys the graduated rate of tax, and only for three years following the death—the "graduated rate estate." Other than this three-year period for one trust, all testamentary trusts are now taxed at the same rate as an *inter vivos* (living) trust, which is the highest marginal rate of tax. Despite these income tax changes, many estates include testamentary trusts, for reasons other than income tax savings. To minimize income taxes year over year, the trust can pay to its beneficiary the income, and the individual beneficiary will continue to enjoy the marginal rate of tax, on all of the beneficiary's income. (In other words, the marginal rate of tax is still available for individuals but can no longer be multiplied with testamentary trusts.) See chapter eight.

Spouse trust

Under the *Income Tax Act*, there is a tax-free "rollover" for a transfer to a spousal (or common law partner) trust, provided both that the spouse is entitled to receive all of the income of the trust during their lifetime, and that no person other than the spouse may receive or otherwise obtain the use of any of the income or capital of the trust before the spouse's death.[1] There should be no provisions disentitling the spouse to all of the income for the remainder of their life, such as if the spouse remarries. A spousal trust is not subject to the twenty-one year deemed disposition rule during the lifetime of the spouse.

Spousal trusts are more common in second marriages, where the will-maker wants their spouse to receive the income from property for the remainder of the spouse's life, but on the spouse's death, the capital is to go to the will-maker's own children. A spousal trust can be difficult for the survivor. If there is a power to encroach on capital for the spouse, the surviving spouse must ask the trustees for an advance. If the trustees include the children of the first spouse, conflicts can arise. The spouse and trustees can also disagree about what mix of investments the trust should hold, such as whether the assets should generate more income at the expense of capital appreciation or vice versa.

---

[1] *Income Tax Act,* R.S.C., 1985, c. 1 (5th Supp.), s70(6).

The spousal trust could be put at risk because of the family property elective rights of the surviving spouse. On the death of their spouse, the surviving married spouse has six months to elect to either receive a "net family property" equalization payment or receive under the terms of the will, in addition to a support claim for married and common law spouses. See chapter seven.

Trusts for children

Many wills include trusts for children. The most common are an individual trust for a particular child or a pooled trust for a group of children. Sometimes, there are successive interests for different beneficiaries over a period of time.

An individual trust for a child is usually created on the death of the will-maker. (The will speaks from the date of death.) Sometimes the child is specifically named in the will, sometimes a child receives a gift because their parent died before the will-maker, and sometimes the child is chosen by a person with the power to appoint which children, among a group of children, should receive a gift. Other times the child's trust is not created until many years after the will-maker dies; for example, a spousal trust which continues until the spouse dies, and then the remainder is distributed equally among the children who are alive at that time.

Most individual trusts give the trustee discretion, i.e. power, to choose whether to transfer income or capital to the child until a stated age. Usually, the trustee is given discretion to either transfer directly to the child or transfer to someone else "for their benefit," which would include tuition payments for the child's school. Some trusts specify that there should be no payments except for specified purposes, such as for the child's education.

Assuming you are the trustee, how should you exercise your discretion? Look to the terms of the trust for guidance. Keep good notes of the decisions made and the reasons for the decisions and make those decisions fairly in consideration of the purpose of the trust. Be careful if someone other than the child is to receive property from the trust in the future. For example, if the trust is for a child for a period, and then to someone else later, you should not personally benefit if the distributions to the first child are minimized.

A pooled trust is where more than one child receives the benefits of the trust for a period. For example, a parent may leave a trust for their children as follows:

> "Hold the remainder of my estate in a trust fund for those of my children who survive me, on the following terms: When the youngest of my children reaches the age of twenty-one, divide the then balance of the fund equally per stirpes among my children and their descendants who are then alive. Before then, you shall use the fund for my children and in the proportions among them as you decide. You need not treat them equally; this is so that you can meet their individual circumstances. You will decide how much of the fund to use, when to use it, and whether to pay amounts to a child or to others on their behalf. You may use income or capital of the fund as you choose…"

How should you exercise your discretion as to sprinkling income and capital among the children before the trust is wound-up? Keep good notes of the decisions made and the reasons for the decisions and make those decisions fairly in consideration of the purpose of the trust fund.

Henson Trust

In a "Henson Trust" the trustees have an absolute discretion to make or withhold payments of income or capital to a person with a disability. In the Ontario *Henson* case,[2] the court held that the disabled person could not compel the trustees to make the payments, and therefore, the disabled person need not include the assets of a Henson Trust when disclosing their liquid assets, for the purpose of calculating their Ontario Disability Support Program ("ODSP") benefits. Thus, the Henson Trust does not limit the income support available. The following is typical wording of a Henson Trust:

> If my son Zane survives me, hold one share in trust for Zane on the following terms (the "fund"). You shall use the fund for Zane while Zane is alive. In your absolute discretion, you will decide how much of the fund to use, when to use it, and whether to pay amounts to Zane or to others on his behalf. You may use income or capital of the fund as you, in your absolute discretion, decide.

---

[2] *Ontario (Ministry of Community and Social Services, Income Maintenance Branch) v. Henson* [1989] O.J. No. 2093 [Ont CA]

The income and capital of the fund shall not vest in Zane and the only interest that Zane shall have shall be the payments actually made to and received by Zane, or to others on his behalf. Without in any way binding your discretion, it is my wish that you maximize the benefits which Zane would receive from other sources if payments from the income and capital of the fund were not paid to Zane or for his own benefit, or if such payments were limited to an amount or time.

[There should be other terms in the trust, such as gift-over if Zane dies, and payments of income after twenty-one years to Zane or to other persons because of the Ontario *Accumulations Act*.]

If you are a trustee of a Henson Trust, how should you use your discretion in making income and capital payments? You should, if possible, ensure that these payments do not disqualify the beneficiary from ODSP benefits by reviewing the regulations under the *Ontario Disability Support Program Act*, which include prescribed limits both for assets and income payments.[3] There are exceptions for a principal residence, a car, student loans, a pre-paid funeral, a Registered Disability Savings Plan, the cash surrender value of life insurance policies, tools of the trade, a loan used for the purchase of an exempt asset, and an interest in a trust derived from an inheritance or life insurance proceeds to a limit of $100,000. These should be carefully considered. Payments to the beneficiary up to certain amounts would not trigger a "claw back" of ODSP benefits. Furthermore, if the assets of the Henson Trust become substantial

[3] In 2020 a person with a disability may not receive payments from trusts in excess of $10,000 over a twelve-month period.

and the disability benefits as compared to the income being earned in the trust are minimal, you could choose to transfer more to the disabled person, and ignore for a period the effect of the claw back. The key, of course, are the terms of the trust (in the above sample, the trustee has the discretion to do this) and the best interests of the beneficiary, including any residuary beneficiary. You should not personally benefit if the distributions to the disabled beneficiary are minimized because of a connection to a residuary beneficiary. Keep good notes of the decisions made and the reasons for the decisions and make those decisions fairly in consideration of the purpose of the Henson Trust.

Charitable remainder trust

A charitable remainder trust is a trust in which income or use of the property is provided to a person during their lifetime, and when they die, the remainder is to be transferred to a named charity. For tax purposes, if an actuary can calculate the expected lifespan of the income beneficiary, and the expected value of the capital of the trust when the income beneficiary dies, and then discount that value in consideration that the charity will not receive the benefit until the future, the charity can issue a tax receipt now, based on the discounted value of the future benefit. In a sense, the gift of capital is made now, but delivery of the gift is postponed. The tax calculations can be complex and professional advice is required.

Charitable gifts and the *cy-pres* doctrine

What if a charity named in the will ceases to exist by the time that the deceased died? Does the gift fail? Similarly, what if the terms of the charitable gift have become impossible or impractical to perform—does the gift fail?

The answer is—probably not. You can apply to the court either to amend the terms of the will so that the gift can be made to a similar charity or to amend the terms of the gift so that the performance of the gift is practical. The key is both establishing an overarching charitable intent, such as a gift to a charity involving certain good deeds and showing the court that amending the terms of the gift would match this overarching charitable intent. An example would be an endowment to a university for students who graduate from a specific program, and after the will was signed, the university merged that program with another program. Most likely, the court would apply the *cy-pres* doctrine and amend the terms of the gift to allow it to be used for the expanded program.

Taxation of a Trust

Taxation of trusts is a complex subject beyond the scope of this handbook. However, a few simple principles can be stated.

With the exception of a graduated rate estates and qualified disability trusts, testamentary trusts (those that arise out of a will) and *inter vivos* trusts (those that are settled by a person still living) are both taxed on their income at the highest marginal rate of tax.

A trust calculates its income (much in the same way as an individual) and then deducts the income that has been paid (or will be paid) to the trust income beneficiaries to arrive at the trust's taxable income (if any). The trust then pays income tax on its taxable income. Unlike an individual, the trust cannot claim the personal income tax credits in calculating its income tax liability. The beneficiaries include the income received or receivable from a trust in their personal income tax returns for the calendar year in which the trust's taxation year ends.

Most income received from a trust retains its character when paid to the beneficiaries who reside in Canada. This means that the beneficiary can claim the dividend tax credit on taxable dividends flowed out of the trust, needs to pay tax on only 50% of capital gains, and can claim foreign tax credits in respect of foreign income received from the trust.

Where the trust has sold an asset in which a capital gains exemption would apply if the asset had been held by an individual, the beneficiary is able to claim the capital gains exemption (assuming the exemption is available to the beneficiary). Capital losses incurred by the trust cannot be used by the trust beneficiaries. The losses are considered to remain in the trust and can be carried forward indefinitely to reduce future capital gains of the trust subject to income tax.

Most amounts paid or payable to non-resident trust beneficiaries are subject to a Canadian income tax withholding. Income such as taxable dividends and capital gains, do not retain their character when paid/payable to non-resident beneficiaries.

Transfer of trust assets to beneficiaries

The passing or transferring of a trust asset to a capital beneficiary does not usually result in an immediate income tax liability for the trust or a capital beneficiary who is a resident of Canada. The trust is considered to have sold the asset to the beneficiary at a selling price (proceeds of disposition) equal to the trust's tax cost (adjusted cost base) of the asset. Therefore, the trust does not incur a capital gain. The beneficiary's tax cost of the assets is equal to the tax cost that the trust had in the asset. The income tax on any accrued gain at the time of transfer – and any accrued gain after the transfer – will be payable once the beneficiary sells the assets or is deemed to have sold the asset such as on death (assuming it is not bequeathed to a surviving spouse) or should the beneficiary become a non-resident of Canada.

Should a trust asset be transferred to a beneficiary who is a non-resident of Canada, the accrued capital gain on the assets will be considered realized and subject to income tax in the trust. This is because the asset is considered to have been disposed of by the trust at a value equal to the fair market value of the asset at the time of transfer.

Each 21st anniversary of a trust

The *Income Tax Act* considers the potential indefinite deferral of income on increases in value of the trust's assets. Generally, a trust is deemed to have disposed of all its assets on every 21st anniversary of its creation (i.e. the settlement of the trust). The deemed disposition triggers the accrued capital gains of the trust property held on that day and income tax is payable on these gains by the trust or the gains can be allocated to the beneficiaries and subject to income tax in their hands.

You can avoid the deemed disposition by transferring the trust's property to its capital beneficiaries prior to the 21st anniversary. If, as noted above, you transfer the trust property to beneficiary resident in Canada, there is no immediate income tax liability.

The deemed disposition rule does not apply to a spousal trust/common-law partner trust, a joint spousal or common-law partner trust, or an alter ego trust.

Chapter 13—Estate Accounting

You must keep detailed financial records and account to the beneficiaries who are to receive a share or percentage of the estate. If these beneficiaries are not satisfied, you must present your accounts to the court on a "passing of accounts". You are not required to account to the legacy beneficiaries, i.e. those who are to receive a specific item or amount of cash; they are only entitled to delivery of their gift. See chapter ten.

Transaction accounting

Estate accounting is transactional. It details the assets at the beginning of the accounting period (the date of death of the deceased), what transactions occurred (receipts and disbursements), and what assets remain at the end of the accounting period. If there are separate income and capital interests to account for, then those transactions are to be recorded separately, as noted below.

Sometimes, accountants present balance sheets and profit and loss statements for an estate, but those statements are not in the best format for estate administration. A balance sheet presents a summary of the assets and liabilities of an entity, including an estate, at a point in time. If the balance sheet lists all the assets and liabilities, rather than just summaries, then the information is useful. A profit and loss statement could be interesting, in that it shows whether the receipts were more than the disbursements, but profit is a business concept for a "going concern," and what estate accounting requires are details of all the receipts and disbursements for an entity being wound up. You are not expected to seek a profit, but to distribute the estate's net assets among the beneficiaries in the proportions required by the will as soon as practicable.

Accounting for separate income and capital interests

For some trusts, you must separately record the income and capital receipts and disbursements. An example is a spousal trust, which could say: "income to my spouse for life, and then capital to my children when she dies". For this trust, you must separate those receipts that are income earned on investments (such as dividends) from those that are based on an increase in the capital value of the investments (accrued capital gains). Similarly, you must separate those disbursements related to earning income from those related to increasing the capital value. The income beneficiary is to receive the income receipts minus the income disbursements.

An example is where the trust owns an apartment building. Rent from the building would be an income receipt. General maintenance expenses and regular repairs would be income disbursements. Take the rental receipts and subtract the income disbursements to calculate the income, which would go to the income beneficiary. If the trust eventually sold the apartment building, the sale price, less all of the costs associated with acquiring, improving and selling the property, would be the capital gain and go to the capital beneficiary.

Getting the beneficiaries to approve the accounts

Unless all the residual beneficiaries otherwise agree, you must "pass" your accounts with the court, i.e. obtain the court's approval to the accounts, for any actions taken, payments made, and compensation claimed. Rather than incurring the expense and delay of going to court, it is best to obtain the approval of all the residuary beneficiaries to the accounts and your compensation claimed. Chapter fifteen describes the steps to wind-up the estate. As part of those steps, you should write to all the residuary beneficiaries and summarize in narrative form the steps you have taken. You should give the beneficiaries a summary of your accounts with a note that details will be provided if requested. It is no coincidence that the position is called estate *trustee*—if you establish trust and show that you can provide supporting invoices and documents for all receipts, disbursements, and steps taken, then usually, the beneficiaries will accept your accounts so that they can receive their inheritance sooner.

Format for estate accounts

If you must pass your accounts with the court, consult the Ontario *Rules of Civil Procedure* for the form of accounts required. You (preferably with the assistance of a lawyer) must file the estate accounts in the format described in Rule 74.17 below:

Rule 74.17 (1) Estate trustees shall keep accurate records of the assets and transactions in the estate and accounts filed with the court shall include:

> (a) on a first passing of accounts, a statement of the assets at the date of death, cross-referenced to entries in the accounts that show the disposition or partial disposition of the assets;

> (b) on any subsequent passing of accounts, a statement of the assets on the date the accounts for the period were opened, cross-referenced to entries in the accounts that show the disposition or partial disposition of the assets, and a statement of the investments, if any, on the date the accounts for the period were opened;

(c) an account of all money received, but excluding investment transactions recorded under clause (e);

(d) an account of all money disbursed, including payments for trustee's compensation and payments made under a court order, but excluding investment transactions recorded under clause (e);

(e) where the estate trustee has made investments, an account setting out,

> (i) all money paid out to purchase investments,

> (ii) all money received by way of repayments or realization on the investments in whole or in part, and

> (iii) the balance of all the investments in the estate at the closing date of the accounts;

(f) a statement of all the assets in the estate that are unrealized at the closing date of the accounts;

(g) a statement of all money and investments in the estate at the closing date of the accounts;

(h) a statement of all the liabilities of the estate, contingent or otherwise, at the closing date of the accounts;

(i) a statement of the compensation claimed by the estate trustee and, where the statement of compensation includes a management fee based on the value of the assets of the estate, a statement setting out the method of determining the value of the assets; and

(j) such other statements and information as the court requires.

(2) The accounts required by clauses (1) (c), (d) and (e) shall show the balance forward for each account.

(3) Where a will or trust deals separately with capital and income, the accounts shall be divided to show separately receipts and disbursements in respect of capital and income.

The estate accounts must be verified by your affidavit in proper form. You must also file a copy of the "Certificate of Appointment of Estate Trustee" and any judgment for any previous passing of accounts (i.e. if there was a previous, interim distribution.)

You must serve the notice of application and a copy of a draft of the judgment sought on each person who has a contingent or vested interest in the estate by regular mail. Rule 74.18 has special requirements for serving the Children's Lawyer on behalf of child beneficiaries and the Public Guardian and Trustee on behalf of adult beneficiaries with a mental disability, as well as other procedural requirements.

Any person served with the notice of application who wishes to object to your accounts shall serve on you, and file with proof of service, a notice of objection to accounts. This objection must be filed at least 35 days before the hearing date specified in the notice of application. The Children's Lawyer or Public Guardian and Trustee must respond at least 30 days before the hearing as to whether they object, request further notice, or will not participate.

If there is an objection that cannot be settled, a hearing is held in the Ontario Superior Court. This can be an expensive procedure, and it is best to isolate which issues are in dispute. Are there payments in dispute? Is there an allegation of negligent administration of the estate? Is there an allegation of favouritism? Is there a dispute about the compensation claimed by the estate trustee? In most cases, it is better to settle than to litigate.

Spreadsheet method for keeping accounts

If you decide to prepare the estate accounts yourself, there are various computer programs available for estate accounting. For simple estates, you can enter the transactions in a spreadsheet program, such as Microsoft Excel or Google Sheets, using the "sheets" function within the program for the different bank and investment accounts, and for the other assets.

This chapter describes a simple spreadsheet to record receipts and disbursements for an estate. It allows you to record the essential information in an easy format duplicating the bank statements received. If the accounts become complicated and a professional review is necessary, the spreadsheet can easily be shared with a professional accountant.

This example spreadsheet can be downloaded for free from the Allen & Allen website, www.allenandallen.ca

www.allenandallen.ca/the-estate-accounting-sample

It is for a fictional estate, and it can be adapted as required. The date of death is assumed to be June 1, 2020.

Chapter one describes how to start with a list of the deceased's assets and liabilities as of the date of death. Enter this information into the first sheet in the spreadsheet.

Assets	Account number	Opening
Chequing account	01-xxxxx	1,500.00
Savings account	02-xxxxx	7,500.00
RRSP account	03-xxxxx	75,000.00
TFSA account	04-xxxxx	50,000.00
Investment account	05-xxxxx	125,000.00
Home	06-xxxxx	750,000.00
Art and paintings	07-xxxxx	1,500.00
Jewelry	08-xxxxx	1,000.00
Car	09-xxxxx	6,000.00
Liabilities		
Line of credit	10-xxxxx	(25,000.00)
Credit card	11-xxxxx	(5,000.00)
Total		987,500.00

Along the bottom of the spreadsheet, there should be links to the separate sheets for each of the listed assets and liabilities. Each of these should link to the corresponding sheet.

For the link to the chequing account, fill in that sheet as follows:

Chequing	01-xxxxx			
Date	Description	Disb't	Rec'd	Balance
June 1, 2020	Opening			1,500.00

"Disb't" is short for "Disbursed" or "Disbursement"
"Rec'd" is short for "Received" or "Receipt"

The amount of $1,500.00 in this cell should be linked to the $1,500.00 in the list of opening assets. In Excel and in Google Sheets, one cell in a computer spreadsheet can be automatically linked to the calculated number from another cell.

As you enter transactions for the period of the estate after death, enter them into the corresponding sheet, and create a formula under the column "Balance" so that it keeps a running balance. The Rec'd column is for all amounts that are added to the bank account, and the Disb't column is for all amounts or values that are deducted from the bank account. The balance should equal the balance in the previous row, plus the receipt in the next row, minus the disbursed in the next row—this formula can be copied all the way down the column. Reconcile your calculated running balance with the bank statement running balance, to be sure that you have entered all the transactions correctly. For bank accounts, you can probably download the transactions and then import them into the spreadsheet.

Chequing	01-xxxxx			
Date	Description	Disb't	Rec'd	Balance
June 1, 2020	Opening			1,500.00
June 3, 2020	CPP received		650.00	2,150.00

Recording the details and categorizing transactions

Return to the particular account sheets and enter columns to the right of the balance column, for the categories of receipts and disbursements. For example, go to the chequing sheet and enter the following categories as columns. These are only suggestions and you may need to create additional columns for different categories of receipts and disbursements:

- Internal (for transfers between estate accounts)
- Property tax
- Income tax
- Funeral
- Medical
- Utilities
- Bank fees
- Insurance
- Pension
- CPP/OAS
- Gain (Loss)
- Distributions

For each receipt and disbursement entered under Disb't and Rec'd, also enter the same amount in one of the columns. In the following example, only the CPP/OAS column is shown because of limited space:

Date	Description	Disb't	Rec'd	Balance	CPP/OAS
June 1, 2020	Opening			1,500.00	
June 3, 2020	CPP received		650.00	2,150.000	650.00

Do this for any transaction entered as a disbursement or receipt; duplicate the number in one of the columns to the right which categorizes the entry. Note: The column for "Internal" is used whenever funds or property is transferred from one estate account to another. For example, if $1,000 is moved from the chequing account to the savings account, the chequing account would have a Disb't of $1,000 and under the Internal column it would show -$1,000 (minus). In the savings account, it would show a Rec'd of $1,000 and a +$1,000 (plus) under the Internal column.

Summarize the categories of expenses

At the end of an accounting period, enter all of the disbursements and receipts and their categories for each sheet. The following is an example for the chequing account:

See next page -

Chequing	01-xxxxx			
Date	Description	Disb't	Rec'd	Balance
June 1, 2020	Opening			1,500.00
June 3, 2020	CPP received		650.00	2,150.00
June 5, 2020	Property tax paid	1,750.00		400.00
June 10, 2020	Pension received		1,250.00	1,650.00
June 15, 2020	Pharmacy paid	75.00		1,575.00
June 18, 2020	Utilities paid	350.00		1,225.00
June 20, 2020	Sale of car - cash rec'vd		5,000.00	6,225.00
June 25, 2020	Insurance paid	85.00		6,140.00
June 29, 2020	Bank fees paid	3.95		6,136.05
		2,263.95	6,900.00	
			Disb't -> (2,263.95)	
	Net increase		4,636.05	

Next is a summary of the categorization of these entries:

Make sure that the net in the first calculation, i.e. $4,636.05, is the same number as the sum of the last row in the categorization. This is to check that you have categorized all the receipts and disbursements.

Note: the two columns on the rights for "Gain (Loss)" and "Distributions" were removed in this list because of limited space.

Internal	Property tax	Income Tax	Medical	Utilities	Bank fees	Insurance	Pension	CPP/OAS
								650.00
	(1,750.00)							
							1,250.00	
			(75.00)					
				(350.00)				
5,000.00								
						(85.00)		
					(3.95)			
5,000.00	(1,750.00)	0.00	(75.00)	(350.00)	(3.95)	(85.00)	1,250.00	650.00
							Sum ->	4,636.05

Do the same for all account sheets during the accounting period.

Entering transactions on the sale of an asset

Suppose the estate had a car estimated to be valued $6,000 at the date of death but was later sold for $5,000. The entries for the car would be as follows:

Car						
Date	Description	Disb't	Rec'd	Balance	Internal	Gain (Loss)
June 1, 2020	Estimated			6,000.00		
June 20, 2020	Sold - asset gone	6,000.00		0.00		(6,000.00)
	Price sold for		5,000.00	5,000.00		5,000.00
June 20, 2020	To chequing	5,000.00		0.00	(5,000.00)	
		11,000.00	5,000.00		(5,000.00)	(1,000.00)
		Disb't ->	(11,000.00)			
	Net decrease		(6,000.00)		Sum ->	(6,000.00)

Although the car was originally estimated to be worth $6,000, it was sold for $5,000 and the cash was put into the chequing account. This sheet is for the car as an asset, so the second line records $6,000 to show that the car has been sold and the asset is gone. The next line shows that it was sold for $5,000. The reason to separate the entries can be seen in the right column, "Gain (Loss)." By entering the transaction in this way, the loss of $1,000 will be part of the summary described below.

The third line shows that the $5,000 was deposited into the chequing account and this is noted as an internal transfer. You must show it as an internal transfer because you cannot claim compensation for transferring cash or an asset from one account to another. Internal transfers should be recorded separately.

Entering the distribution of jewelry

This is what you do with an asset, such as jewelry, that is distributed directly to the beneficiaries rather than sold for cash like the car.

Jewelry					
Date	Description	Disb't	Rec'd	Balance	Distributions
June 1, 2020	Estimated			1,000.00	
June 20, 2020	Distributed	1,000.00		-	(1,000.00)
		1,000.00	-		
		Disb't ->	(1,000.00)		
	Net decrease		(1,000.00)		(1,000.00)

Entering the payment of a liability

Suppose on June 22, 2020 you transfer $5,000 from the savings account to pay-off the outstanding credit card balance. The following would be the entries for the savings account:

Savings	02-xxxxx				
Date	Description	Disb't	Rec'd	Balance	Internal
June 1, 2020	Opening			7,500.00	
June 22, 2020	Payment of credit card debt	5,000.00		2,500.00	(5,000.00)

The following would be the corresponding entries for the credit card account:

Credit card	12-xxxxx				
Date	Description	Disb't	Rec'd	Balance	Internal
June 1, 2020	Opening			(5,000.00)	
June 22, 2020	Payment of credit card debt		5,000.00	0.00	5,000.00

Entering investment account information

Investment accounts (held by a financial institution) will include detailed information of investments purchased and sold, the dividends and interest payments received, fees charged, and deposits and withdrawals of cash from the account by the estate. If there are separate interests for the income and capital beneficiaries in the trust (such as "income to my spouse for life, and then capital to my children when she dies"), you must enter all of this information in your spreadsheet and track income and capital separately. To do this, you may need to purchase a more sophisticated program. If, however, the income is added to the capital and distributed to the beneficiaries (which is usually the case for an estate), you need not track income and capital separately. This example spreadsheet does not track income and capital separately.

If income and capital are not tracked separately, rather than repeat the investment account information, which can be difficult to download to your computer, you could add the total monthly receipts and disbursement in the investment account and enter the summary monthly, with a reference to the source documents. You will need to track (a) all money received by way of the sale of investments in whole or in part and deposits made, and (b) the balance of all the investments in the estate at the closing date of the accounts.

Updating "Current" values.

The current values column in the list of assets and liabilities should be updated, by linking the column to the current balances in each of the accounts.

Assets	Account number	Opening	Current
Chequing account	01-xxxxx	1,500.00	6,136.05
Savings account	02-xxxxx	7,500.00	2,500.00
RRSP account	03-xxxxx	75,000.00	75,000.00
TFSA account	04-xxxxx	50,000.00	50,000.00
Investment account	05-xxxxx	125,000.00	125,000.00
Home	06-xxxxx	750,000.00	750,000.00
Art and paintings	07-xxxxx	1,500.00	1,500.00
Jewelry	08-xxxxx	1,000.00	0.00
Car	09-xxxxx	6,000.00	0.00
Liabilities			
Line of credit	10-xxxxx	(25,000.00)	(25,000.00)
Credit card	11-xxxxx	(5,000.00)	0.00
Total		987,500.00	985,136.05

As time progresses, add new sheets for new accounts that are opened, such as an estate account at the bank.

Summarize all the receipts and disbursements

Create a new sheet after the "Assets and Liabilities" sheet and call it "Receipts and Disbursements." In that new sheet, make rows for each of the categories that were used in the various sheets, and make columns for the different accounts. On the next page is our example so far. You can obtain a clearer view of this sheet by downloading the spreadsheet from:

www.allenandallen.ca/the-estate-accounting-sample

	Chequing	Savings	RRSP	TFSA	Investment	Home	Art	Jewelry	Car	Line of credit	Credit Card	Totals
Opening assets	$ 1,500.00	$ 7,500.00	$ 75,000.00	$ 50,000.00	$ 125,000.00	$ 750,000.00	$ 1,500.00	$ 1,000.00	$ 6,000.00	$ (25,000.00)	$ (5,000.00)	$ 987,500.00
Internal transfers	$ 5,000.00	$ (5,000.00)	$ -	$ -	$ -	$ -	$ -	$ -	$ (5,000.00)	$ -	$ 5,000.00	$ -
Property tax	$ (1,750.00)	$ -	$ -	$ -	$ -	$ -	$ -	$ -	$ -	$ -	$ -	$ (1,750.00)
Income tax	$ -	$ -	$ -	$ -	$ -	$ -	$ -	$ -	$ -	$ -	$ -	$ -
Funeral	$ -	$ -	$ -	$ -	$ -	$ -	$ -	$ -	$ -	$ -	$ -	
Medical	$ (75.00)	$ -	$ -	$ -	$ -	$ -	$ -	$ -	$ -	$ -	$ -	$ (75.00)
Utilities	$ (350.00)	$ -	$ -	$ -	$ -	$ -	$ -	$ -	$ -	$ -	$ -	$ (350.00)
Bank fees	$ (3.95)	$ -	$ -	$ -	$ -	$ -	$ -	$ -	$ -	$ -	$ -	$ (3.95)
Insurance	$ (85.00)	$ -	$ -	$ -	$ -	$ -	$ -	$ -	$ -	$ -	$ -	$ (85.00)
Pension	$ 1,250.00	$ -	$ -	$ -	$ -	$ -	$ -	$ -	$ -	$ -	$ -	$ 1,250.00
CPP / OAS	$ 650.00	$ -	$ -	$ -	$ -	$ -	$ -	$ -	$ -	$ -	$ -	$ 650.00
Gain (Loss)	$ -	$ -	$ -	$ -	$ -	$ -	$ -	$ (1,000.00)	$ -	$ -	$ -	$ (1,000.00)
Distributions	$ -	$ -	$ -	$ -	$ -	$ -	$ -	$ -	$ (1,000.00)	$ -	$ -	$ (1,000.00)
Current values	$ 6,136.05	$ 2,500.00	$ 75,000.00	$ 50,000.00	$ 125,000.00	$ 750,000.00	$ 1,500.00	$ -	$ -	$ (25,000.00)	$ -	$ 985,136.05

Opening	$ 987,500.00
Receipt-Disbursements	$ (2,363.95)
Current (reconciled)	$ 985,136.05

Summarize the records for an accounting

The last column of the preceding summary table allows you to summarize for the beneficiaries a simple accounting.

	Totals
Opening assets	987,500.00
Internal transfers (this can be deleted; it should always be zero)	0.00
Property tax paid	(1,750.00)
Income tax	0.00
Funeral	0.00
Medical – pharmacy paid	(75.00)
Utilities paid	(350.00)
Bank fees paid	(3.95)
Insurance paid	(85.00)
Pension received	1,250.00
CPP / OAS received	650.00
Gain (Loss) on sale of car	(1,000.00)
Distributions (jewelry)	(1,000.00)
Current values	985,136.05

You can include this summary in a letter to the beneficiaries, setting out the net assets you started with, a summary of the receipts, a summary of the disbursements, and the net assets at the end of the accounting period. Any beneficiary who requests further details can be given them, including copies of bank, investment account, and credit card statements.

133

Chapter Fourteen—Compensation for the Estate Trustee

You are entitled to be paid for administering the estate. How much compensation you are entitled to and when you may receive it is governed by the will, statutes, and the common law. Most wills are silent on the issue. This is because it can be difficult for the will-maker to know at the time of signing their will which assets will need to be administered and how complicated the job will be after they die. For example, someone in their fifties may have illiquid assets, such as ownership of a timeshare in Florida, a cottage, an operating business, intellectual property, options and shares, which, by the time they die, will have been converted to a liquid portfolio of investments. Some estates involve litigation (for example, from disappointed beneficiaries who allege undue influence, from spouses or children who claim dependant support, from creditors who claim questionable debts, and complex tax litigation). The amount of work and the expertise required may be difficult to predict.

Section 61(1) of the Ontario *Trustee Act* states that a "personal representative [i.e. estate trustee] is entitled to such fair and reasonable allowance for the care, pains and trouble, and the time expended in and about the estate, as may be allowed by a judge of the Superior Court of Justice."

This, of course, does not provide much guidance. Fortunately, case law has developed a "rule of thumb" for total compensation to administer an estate, being 2.5% of receipts, 2.5% of disbursements (i.e. 5% of the gross value of the estate), plus an annual "care and management fee" of 2/5 of 1% of the average value of assets invested and managed for an ongoing testamentary trust. But some estates require less work than others, and this "rule of thumb" may be inappropriate. For example, if the estate consists of one asset—an investment account of $10 million—and there is no litigation or difficulty in determining the beneficiaries, then 5% or $500,000 compensation would be excessive.

Therefore, in determining whether the tariff calculation is "fair and reasonable," courts generally have regard to these five factors:

- the size of the estate;
- the care and responsibility involved;
- the time occupied in performing the duties;
- the skill and ability shown by the estate trustee; and
- the degree of success resulting from the administration.

You are entitled to reimbursement for necessary legal fees, tax filing fees, and out-of-pocket expenses. However, fees paid to an accountant or other professional to review and/or report on the estate accounts should be deducted from your compensation; otherwise, the beneficiaries are effectively paying twice for the same administrative work.

You cannot take compensation unless either all of the beneficiaries agree, or the court approves the amount of compensation on a passing of accounts. See chapter thirteen. "Pre-taking" compensation is not permitted, unless the will or trust document specifically authorizes it.[1] Good practice is to keep the beneficiaries advised of all developments in the administration of the estate, to obtain their approval to an interim distribution, and to reserve a sufficient amount

---

[1] *Re Knoch*, [1982] O.J. No. 2516, 12 E.T.R. 162, 1982 CarswellOnt 622 (Surr. Ct.).

of funds until a tax clearance certificate is obtained from the Canada Revenue Agency confirming that all income taxes have been paid.

Sharing the compensation

The total compensation is what is approved by the court or the beneficiaries. If there is more than one estate trustee, you and the other estate trustees must agree about how to share the compensation. You should also agree about how to share the work. This agreement should be put in writing. If you cannot come to an agreement you must obtain an order from the court about sharing the compensation. The cost of the court application should be paid by the estate trustees and not by the beneficiaries.

Income tax considerations

Your estate trustee compensation is taxable, so if you are also a beneficiary of the estate you are administering, you should consider waiving compensation because there is no income tax in Canada for the recipient of an inheritance. Note: you cannot disguise compensation by bartering with the other beneficiaries to transfer a portion of their inheritance to you in lieu of taxable compensation.

If you are administering the estate as an individual estate trustee, your compensation is treated like a salary payment and withholdings for CPP and income tax are required, and the estate is to issue a T4. The estate would need to open a "payroll account" with Canada Revenue Agency. It is best to seek an accountant for advice.

If you are in the *business* of providing advice, the fee is considered "business income" (either earned as self-employment income or through a corporation) and HST may be chargeable on top of the fee.

Approving the accounts of a previous attorney under a power of attorney

If the deceased was elderly or incapacitated, their attorney for property may have handled their finances for a period. If so, the attorney (who need not be a lawyer) may request that the estate pay them for their work for the period before the deceased died. Before approving these accounts and paying them from the estate, you should review the accounts and the steps taken by the attorney, bearing in mind that an attorney has obligations under the Ontario *Substitute Decisions Act*.

When reviewing the attorney's accounting, keep in mind that gifts or loans to the incapable person's friends or relatives may be made only if there is reason to believe, based on intentions the person expressed before becoming incapable, that he or she would make them if capable.[2] Charitable gifts may be made only if the incapable person authorized the making of charitable gifts in a power of attorney executed before becoming incapable or there is evidence that the person made similar expenditures when capable. The total amount or value of charitable gifts shall not exceed the lesser of twenty percent of the income of the property in the year in which the gifts are made and the maximum amount or value of charitable gifts provided for in a power of attorney executed by the incapable person before becoming incapable.[3]

---

[2] *Substitute Decisions Act*, 1992, S.O. 1992, c. 30, s 37.
[3] *Ibid.*

The power of attorney can state how much the attorney will be paid. If it doesn't, the fees are prescribed by regulation. At present, the fees are three percent on income and capital receipts; three percent on income and capital disbursements; and three-fifths of one percent on the annual average value of the assets as a care and management fee.[4]

---

[4] *Ontario Regulation 26/95.*

Chapter 15—Winding up the Estate

If you have completed your accounting (chapter thirteen) and have decided on the amount of compensation to claim (chapter fourteen), then you are then ready to deliver your final report and distribution plan to the beneficiaries. You may have already done an interim distribution and been paid interim compensation with the approval of the beneficiaries, with a holdback for debts and for the tax clearance certificate. You will have distributed the personal effects, filed the personal and estate income tax returns, dealt with any possible litigation, and set up any ongoing trusts.

Proposing the final distribution

The legacy gifts should have all been paid, so it is a matter of reporting to the remainder beneficiaries. If you have already sent an interim distribution report, consider doing a summary accounting from the date of the interim report to the date of the final report. Alternatively, you could do a complete report and indicate that everything to the end of the interim has already been approved.

You should *not* do a final report until you have the tax clearance certificate.

One option is to do the final report in narrative format, describing in chronological order how the estate was administered, what issues arose, and how they were dealt with. If any transaction required judgment, then include copies of the professional appraisal reports and advice about income taxes, estate administration tax, litigation, and other important issues. The level of detail required will depend on how much the beneficiaries want. It is better to provide too much information, rather than not enough.

For the accounting, take the summary column and include it in your reporting letter. At the end of chapter thirteen is a summary accounting, a copy of which is located below. Obviously, these numbers would be different in the final report which is why in this example they are blank. In a separate sheet, you can explain how you calculated your compensation.

	Totals
Opening assets	$987,500.00
Internal transfers (this can be deleted; it should be zero)	$0.00
Property tax paid	
Income tax paid	
Funeral paid	
Medical (Pharmacy) paid	
Utilities paid	
Bank fees paid	
Insurance paid	
Pension received	
CPP / OAS received	
Gain (Loss) on sale of assets	
Distributions	
Current values	
Compensation claimed	
Available for distribution	

Obtain final releases before distributing

Just as with the interim distribution, obtain releases from all residual beneficiaries before distributing any funds. This encourages the beneficiaries to contact each other to sign releases, since no one will receive until all approve.

On receipt of $***** the undersigned, John Fiction.

Approves the accounting and final distribution proposal of the Estate Trustee set out in a Summary dated December 30, 2020, for the period since Jack Fiction died on June 1, 2020 to the date of December 30, 2020;

Releases and discharges the Estate Trustee, her agents, associates and representatives, successors and assigns of and from any and all actions, causes of actions, claims, demands for damages or loss, however arising, including all claims for costs including all damage or loss which may arise in the future, arising from all matters having to do with the administration of the Estate for the period from June 1, 2020 to the date of December 30, 2020.

I confirm that I have been provided full disclosure of the accounts of the Estate to the date of December 30, 2020, with access to all supporting documents to support the summary.

I confirm that I have been advised to retain independent legal advice before signing this release.

Once you have all the releases, send the beneficiaries their funds. You can do cheques or bank transfers, as you wish.

Concluding remarks

We hope that being an estate trustee was a role that you found fulfilling. The deceased chose you to look after their affairs, and if you have done so in keeping with their intentions as expressed in their will, then you will have honoured their legacy.

Manufactured by Amazon.ca
Bolton, ON

25672118R00088